PROVERBS

Published by
The Bible Reading Fellowship
Sandy Lane West, Oxford, England
ISBN 1 84101 071 5

First edition 1999
10 9 8 7 6 5 4 3 2 1 0

Acknowledgments
Unless otherwise stated, scripture quotations are taken from The
New Revised Standard Version of the Bible, Anglicized Edition,
copyright © 1989, 1995 by the Division of Christian Education of
the National Council of the Churches of Christ in the United States
of America, and are used by permission.
The Revised Standard Version of the Bible, copyright © 1946, 1952,
1971 by the Division of Christian Education of the National Council
of the Churches of Christ in the United States of America, and are
used by permission.
New English Bible with the Apocrypha: Oxford Study Edition
copyright © 1976 by Oxford Univerity Press, Inc.
Revised English Bible with the Apocrypha copyright © 1989 by
Oxford University Press and Cambridge University Press.
Extracts from the Authorized Version of the Bible (The King James
Bible), the rights in which are vested in the Crown, are reproduced
by permission of the Crown's Patentee, Cambridge University Press.
Extracts from The Book of Common Prayer of 1662, the rights of
which are vested in the Crown in perpetuity within the United
Kingdom, are reproduced by permission of Cambridge University
Press, Her Majesty's Printers.
Extracts from *The Alternative Service Book 1980* are copyright © The
Archbishops' Council and are reproduced by permission.
Material from *Celebrating Common Prayer* (Mowbray), © The Society
of Saint Francis 1992, is used with permission.

A catalogue record for this book is available
from the British Library

Printed and bound in Great Britain
by Caledonian Manufacturing International, Glasgow

PROVERBS

THE PEOPLE'S
BIBLE COMMENTARY

ENID B.
MELLOR

A BIBLE COMMENTARY FOR EVERY DAY

The Bible Reading Fellowship
OPENING THE BIBLE

INTRODUCING THE
PEOPLE'S BIBLE COMMENTARY
SERIES

Congratulations! You are embarking on a voyage of discovery—or rediscovery. You may feel you know the Bible very well; you may never have turned its pages before. You may be looking for a fresh way of approaching daily Bible study; you may be searching for useful insights to share in a study group or from a pulpit.

The People's Bible Commentary (PBC) series is designed for all those who want to study the scriptures in a way that will warm the heart as well as instructing the mind. To help you, the series distils the best of scholarly insights into the straightforward language and devotional emphasis of Bible reading notes. Explanation of background material, and discussion of the original Greek and Hebrew, will always aim to be brief.

- If you have never really studied the Bible before, the series offers a serious yet accessible way in.

- If you help to lead a church study group, or are otherwise involved in regular preaching and teaching, you can find invaluable 'snapshots' of a Bible passage through the PBC approach.

- If you are a church worker or minister, burned out on the Bible, this series could help you recover the wonder of scripture.

Using a People's Bible Commentary

The series is designed for use alongside any version of the Bible. You may have your own favourite translation, but you might like to consider trying a different one in order to gain fresh perspectives on familiar passages.

Many Bible translations come in a range of editions, including study and reference editions that have concordances, various kinds of special index, maps and marginal notes. These can all prove helpful in studying the relevant passage. The Notes section at the back of each PBC volume provides space for you to write personal reflections, points to follow up, questions and comments.

Each People's Bible Commentary can be used on a daily basis, instead of Bible reading notes. Alternatively, it can be read straight through, or used as a resource book for insight into particular verses of the biblical book.

If you have enjoyed using this commentary and would like to progress further in Bible study, you will find details of other volumes in the series listed at the back, together with information about a special offer from BRF.

While it is important to deepen understanding of a given passage, this series always aims to engage both heart and mind in the study of the Bible. The scriptures point to our Lord himself and our task is to use them to build our relationship with him. When we read, let us do so prayerfully, slowly, reverently, expecting him to speak to our hearts.

CONTENTS

PBC PROVERBS: INTRODUCTION

We might expect a book called 'Proverbs' to consist of wise sayings about everyday life—like 'A stitch in time saves nine', or 'Too many cooks spoil the broth'. Proverbs includes plenty of this sort of thing: the *mashal*, a terse and often witty saying, was part of Hebrew literature. There are religious proverbs—'The fear of the Lord is the beginning of knowledge' (1:7); practical advice—'Do not wear yourself out to get rich; be wise enough to desist' (23:4); and a few sayings which have in some form survived into the present—'Do not boast about tomorrow, for you do not know what a day may bring' (27:1).

However, there is more than this to the book of Proverbs. For one thing, there are far too many proverbs to remember, and they extend beyond everyday life—for example:

In the light of a King's face there is life,
and his favour is like the clouds that bring the spring rain (16:15).

For another, they are written as poetry—perhaps because poetry is easier to memorize than prose, or perhaps to give added weight to literature that claims neither the authority of law nor the urgency of prophecy. 'Like a gold ring or an ornament of gold is a wise rebuke to a listening ear' (25:12) is certainly more impressive than, as we might say, 'A word to the wise'.

But perhaps most important is the fact that the book is part of a much larger body of writing called 'Wisdom Literature'.

'Wisdom' in the Old Testament means, basically, the ability to cope. It can take different forms: good craftsmanship (Exodus 28:3), good administration (Deuteronomy 1:13), intellectual brilliance (1 Kings 4:29ff.) or shrewd common sense (1 Kings 3:16–28). It always implies assessing a situation and acting for the best, and so it is linked not only with expediency but also with right and wrong, and ultimately with the will of God. In the later Old Testament, and in the period between the Testaments, there seems to have been a class of 'wise men' who would advise anyone who came to their 'house of learning' (see Ecclesiasticus 51:23, NEB), and collections of their sayings are preserved in the 'Wisdom books'—Job, Proverbs and Ecclesiastes in the Old Testament; Ecclesiasticus, the Wisdom of Solomon and Tobit in the Apocrypha.

Wisdom literature may consist of short sayings or longer reflections on the meaning of life—the book of Job grapples with the mystery of innocent suffering, while Ecclesiastes asks, 'What is the point of it all?'—or a mixture of the two. Sometimes wisdom is described as a person; the Law, providing a framework for a well-ordered life (Ecclesiasticus 24:1–23); or a divine agent who took part in the work of creation (Proverbs 8:22–31).

However, wisdom and 'the wise' are not peculiar to the Bible. They appear, for example, in the literature of ancient Egypt. Ptah-hotep, chief counsellor to the Pharaoh of the time, was writing as early as 2450BC. He distilled for his son what he had learnt from the experience of a lifetime. 'For,' he says, 'there is no one born wise.' A much later work, believed to have come from Thebes and now in the British Museum, its suggested dates ranging from 1300BC to 600BC, is likewise addressed by a father to his son. *The Teaching of Amen-em-opet*, like that of Ptah-hotep, contains sayings which are strikingly like Proverbs. For example, Amen-em-opet says, 'Do not associate to thyself the heated man, nor visit him for conversation', while Proverbs 22:24 advises, 'Make no friends with those given to anger, and do not associate with hotheads.'

So how is wisdom in the Bible different from, say, Egyptian wisdom? All biblical wisdom comes from God, and offers a way of life which the gods of ancient Egypt do not offer. And the fulfilment of these interwoven and developing ideas of wisdom is in the New Testament, where Jesus is 'the power of God and the wisdom of God' (1 Corinthians 1:24).

Reading Proverbs

How can we make sense of these long chapters of sayings dealing with topics ranging from animals to wealth, and from parents, education and discipline to bribery and drunkenness, mixed with passages which build up a portrait of Wisdom as a person?

This is not a book to be read at one sitting. First we need to realize that it contains different kinds of writing by different authors. The opening words are 'The proverbs of Solomon son of David, king of Israel', and chapter 25 begins, 'These are other proverbs of Solomon that the officials of King Hezekiah of Judah copied.' We know that Solomon was famous for his wisdom, but other sections are attributed to other authors—Agur (30:1), Lemuel (31:1), and an unnamed group called 'the wise' (22:17). No doubt these collections of sayings were edited and re-edited, and what we have is the last of several versions, the final editor unknown. Sometimes we shall find that the Hebrew for a particular verse or word is different from its Greek translation. The earliest complete 'official' Hebrew Bible dates from the tenth century AD, so those manuscripts are copies, made hundreds of years after the books themselves were written, and, in spite of the Hebrew scholars' reputation for accuracy, there are variations between copies. A letter, a word or a sentence may vary, or words may be in a different order.

Much older than the Hebrew 'received' Bible, as it is called, is the Greek version, known as the Septuagint (from the Latin for 'seventy') because according to tradition it was translated by seventy-two scholars at Alexandria in the third century BC, and likewise based on documents which are lost.

When we add the ancient translations into Aramaic, Syriac and other languages, plus the amount of editing which must have been undertaken, it is remarkable that the discrepancies are so few, rather than so many.

It is sometimes said that Proverbs was written for a social élite, perhaps the young men of Israel who were being trained up as future leaders; it certainly shows knowledge of life at Court, while on the other hand the 'poor' are never addressed directly, but seen as those to be cared for by society. Yet its concerns are universal—food, shelter, work, leisure, sex and marriage, the management of relationships, business, health, death. There is something for everyone.

To get the best out of Proverbs without being daunted by its complexity, it helps if we use our imaginations to visualize and identify with the real-life situations behind the sayings and to appreciate and learn from the characters that cross the stage—the schoolboy and the parent, the absent husband and the unfaithful woman, the gossip and the royal messenger, the farmer, the courtier, and the rest. Many of these situations, together with some of the warnings about, for example, drunkenness and unfaithfulness, speak directly to today's society, and it is difficult to remember that Proverbs was written so long ago.

A sense of humour also comes in handy. 'Like somebody who takes a passing dog by the ears is one who meddles in the quarrel of another' (26:17) is as funny as it is true.

But above all we need to pray for spiritual discernment as we enjoy the variety which Proverbs provides. Not all the sayings are overtly spiritual, but all show us people facing up to the problem that confronts everyone—how to live and work in the world, while acknowledging God's claim on, and trusting in his guidance for, their lives. Remember that even in its most down-to-earth moments, Proverbs is grounded in a sure faith in God.

However, there is a problem about the benefits of this faith which Proverbs promises. There is a lot of emphasis on riches and worldly advancement as the reward for a life of obedience, and the literal interpretation of these verses is reflected in the contemporary 'prosperity gospel', which stresses the material blessings given to the faithful, in contrast with the simple life that Jesus led and expected his followers to observe. While we cannot at this distance read the writers' minds, it may help to remember that the Old Testament does not teach anything definite about life after death, so any benefits for the godly had to be envisaged in the context of earthly life, and were to be shared with others less fortunate (see 1 Chronicles 29:10–14).

Among the sayings in chapters 1—9, we see the emerging portrait of Wisdom as an individual. She is portrayed as a woman: outspoken (1:20), attractive (2:10–15), and a life-enhancer (3:13–18). She is just (8:20), and supremely worth getting to know (4:1–9). Above all, she personifies the principle by which God ordered the world (3:19–20) in the work of creation (8:22–31). Realistically, after the sublime picture in chapter 8 there is the contrast between Wisdom and another woman, Folly—ignorant, loud-mouthed, appealing to the 'simple' (men without moral insight) who accept her invitation to her house but who 'do not know that the dead are there' (9:18). There are warnings to heed as well as examples to follow. In the period between the Old and New Testaments, Wisdom, like the Word of God, began to take on some of the attributes of God himself, and this increasing tendency not only to set Wisdom beside God but in some sense to identify the two, helped to prepare the way for understanding Jesus, 'the wisdom of God' (1 Corinthians 1:24).

1   PROVERBS 1:1–7

WHAT *is it* ALL ABOUT?

'The proverbs of Solomon son of David, king of Israel' (v. 1) is probably meant as the introduction to the whole book, but verses 2–7 are in fact a preface to chapters 1—9, the first section of Proverbs. Its purpose is described in various ways: 'for learning', 'for understanding', 'for gaining instruction', 'to teach', 'to understand', add up to one comprehensive word—'education'.

Who is to be educated?

The young (v. 4), at a time of life when they are particularly vulnerable, and the 'simple' (v. 4)—a word probably meaning the inexperienced or easily led, open to both wisdom and foolishness.

But education is also for 'the wise' (v. 5). It does not end when we grow up. It is a lifelong process; there is always more to learn.

How does it happen?

It happens by various methods. Instruction (v. 2) has an element of discipline—we must apply ourselves. 'To teach' (v. 4) means to set something before us: that is, 'the words of the wise' (v. 6)—a good teacher is the most powerful force in education—and proverbs, riddles and figures (v. 6). 'Proverbs' here means short, easily remembered sayings. Riddles (such as Proverbs 1:17) were a form of entertainment with a serious side—Solomon had to answer the 'hard questions' (the same word) which the Queen of Sheba came to ask him (1 Kings 10:1). Learning through riddles is something like exercises in problem-solving. 'Figures' (such as Proverbs 7:6–23) are stories or parables, which have to be interpreted. So the education offered is by straight instruction and through active participation.

What is the curriculum?

It is not concerned with the three 'R's, but with personal growth—what nowadays would appear on a timetable as 'Religious, Personal, Social and Moral Education'.

'Wise dealing' (v. 3) implies intelligently assessing a situation and acting appropriately, and it can manifest itself in different ways. 'Righteousness', which is true and just, one of the attributes of God himself; justice, or moral accuracy in making decisions; and equity, or uprightness (v. 3), are spiritual and moral virtues. Others are more practical: shrewdness—being streetwise enough to look after oneself; knowledge—information acquired and put to good use; prudence, or discretion; and skill—a word connected with pulling on a rope while steering a ship, here meaning a right sense of direction (vv. 4–5).

And the outcome?

This education aims to produce more than ability and integrity. Its goal is that the students shall know 'the fear of the Lord' (v. 7); not terror, but reverent obedience to the standards which God requires. This is where true knowledge (and so true wisdom) begin; there is no other way to acquire it. Only the fools seal their own fate by their own behaviour, being incorrigible, unlike the 'simple', who are open to guidance.

PRAYER

Teach me, my God and King
In all things thee to see.
And what I do in anything
To do it as for thee.

George Herbert (1593–1632)

FATHERLY ADVICE (I)

In the first nine chapters of Proverbs there are ten passages beginning 'my child' or 'my children', usually translated 'my son(s)', but in fact applicable to both sexes and all ages. They follow the pattern of traditional teaching of the time—the address, 'my child'; an instruction to pay attention; the main message, usually an exhortation or a command; and finally a reflection on the happy outcome of following the advice and/or the misery of those who reject it.

However, the references to the mother's influence here (v. 8) and elsewhere (4:3; 6:20) suggest that in Israel education was not left to the professionals, but was an important part of the life in the home. This is reinforced by Deuteronomy 6:6–7: 'Keep these words that I am commanding you today in your heart. Recite them to your children and talk about them when you are at home and when you are away, when you lie down and when you rise'.

Any teacher will tell you that in spite of parents' sometimes unrealistic expectations of the school, by far the most powerful influence on a child is that of the home. The particular problem on which the following verses concentrate is peer pressure (vv. 10–14).

The danger of joining the gang

Verses 10–14 were probably intended in the first place for young men who had left their villages to seek a living in Jerusalem with its noisy streets and its violent underclass (already mentioned by earlier prophets such as Amos, Hosea and Micah, who all describe the systematic and indeed legalized exploitation of the poor by the rich). Hijacking, looting, even murder, were financially profitable and also offered the excitement of living dangerously. The sense of power over a victim was like the power of Sheol, the place of the dead, which greedily and inexorably swallowed up its victims.

The anxiety expressed here must strike a chord with many present-day parents whose adolescent children are leaving home. Will the 'fair garland' (v. 9)—the attractiveness of the home with its standards and stability—be a match for peer pressure, for the flattering invitation to adopt the lifestyle of 'sinners' (literally 'those who miss the mark' and so fail to achieve any worthwhile aim in life)? Unthinking and utterly self-concerned, they have no idea of the fate which eventually awaits them when they are caught and suffer the consequences of their actions; they are even more foolish than birds, who at least avoid an obvious trap (v. 17).

How can we help young people to see that the unthinking 'gang mentality' may bring immediate gratification, but that its long-term effects can be disastrously destructive in terms both of retribution and of the loss of self-respect? Perhaps the first step is to admit that it involves us too.

This is for us all

It is easy to shake our heads over the temptations and wrongdoing of the young, but we are all made in the image of God, which means the image of the Trinity, that perfect partnership of diversity in unity. So the choice of our friends and the quality of our relationships affect us in the long as well as the short term. When we look back, will our life story include incidents and intimacies which have had a destructive effect? Do we need to ask forgiveness for our own shortcomings in relation to others, before we try to convince younger people that both individual and group friendships are part of a long process, helping to form our characters, and leading to the way of life or to the path of disaster?

TO THINK ABOUT

Now, though Solomon specifies only the temptations to rob on the highways yet he intends hereby to warn us against all other evils which sinners entice men to.

Matthew Henry (1662–1714)

How much are we influenced by others? How often are we swayed by the desire to be popular, to be tolerant, to be up-to-date in our thinking and lifestyle?

PRAYER

Lord, help me not to be 'conformed to this world', but to be transformed by the renewing of my mind, so that I may discern what is the will of God—what is good and acceptable and perfect.
(Romans 12:2)

WISDOM'S PORTRAIT (I)

Proverbs is not short of female figures, though not all of them might please a feminist! There is the mother (1:8; 6:20), the beloved young wife (5:18–19), the queen telling her son how to behave as king (31:1–9). There is the capable, experienced matriarch (31:10–31), and, by way of contrast, the noisy, vulgar yet plausible seducer (5:3–9 and elsewhere). But among these women Wisdom is the dominant and probably the most intriguing figure, perhaps because there is an air of mystery about her. Sometimes we catch a glimpse like a rough pencil sketch, sometimes we have a three-dimensional portrait in full colour, sometimes Wisdom herself speaks, sometimes the writer describes something about her. But as soon as we are getting to know her, she retreats.

Although the idea of Wisdom appears elsewhere in the literature of the ancient Near East, we find her as a person only in Israelite writings. We need to remember that underlying even her most down-to-earth teaching is the understanding that she is part of God's order of things and that to be 'wise' in listening to her involves loving obedience to God's commands.

A public speech

Here, Wisdom speaks (v. 20), and is up-front with her message; she holds forth in 'the street... the squares... the busiest corner'—above all, in the gate of the city where business is transacted and judgment is pronounced by the elders. She is no shrinking violet: she can hold her own with the men who rule the city, and there is nothing private about what she has to say. It is public, demanding and noisy. What is it all about, and why should anyone listen?

A question and an appeal

Why are the 'simple' so unwilling to take notice (vv. 20–23)? The simple, or naïve, ones are the young whose characters are not yet formed by education and training. They are not insolent or contemptuous like those in verse 30, but they are heedless, facetious and at the same time vulnerable. So it is urgent that they should hear what

Wisdom has to say before they are corrupted by other influences. How can Wisdom reach them?

Finding ways to help and guide the young is an absolute priority; change is so much harder later in life.

A reproof and a warning

Wisdom's severest words are for those who should know better (vv. 24–32). They have ignored and rejected her, and have shown her nothing but contempt. But she will have the last laugh when things go disastrously wrong for them—as they will (vv. 24–27); and when they try to put things right it will be too late. Verse 28 is a frightening reverse image of God's offer, 'I held out my hands all day long to a rebellious people' (Isaiah 65:2). The pig-headed and the know-alls will have their way—and live to regret it (vv. 30–32). They will destroy themselves, and have only themselves to blame. Worst of all, saying 'No' to Wisdom means saying 'No' to God (v. 29).

Another way

There is no need to rush into disaster. Wisdom's way is to listen to God and to obey him. Then troubled lives will know security, because they will be at peace with themselves (v. 33). Today we tend to want instant solutions to our problems—usually proposed by ourselves or other people. Believing prayer and quiet reflection are better ways of ensuring effective decisions and inward peace.

TO THINK ABOUT

*Do not be deceived; God is not mocked, for you reap
whatever you sow. If you sow to your own flesh,
you will reap corruption from the flesh; but if you sow to the Spirit,
you will reap eternal life from the Spirit.*
(Galatians 6:7–8)

FATHERLY ADVICE (II)

The piece of teaching which takes up chapter 2 is in two parts: verses 1–9, which make clear the connection between wisdom and God, and the rest of the chapter, which warns about the likely consequences of foolishness and defiance.

There is a humility about the father's approach here. The 'words' are his commandments—he does not pretend to be a prophet who says, 'Thus says the Lord'. Nor does he claim that his instructions are the Law with a capital L—rather, they are the fruit of thought and experience, perhaps coming from 'the wise' who figure in this part of the Old Testament.

The voice of experience is not to be ignored, but we have to ask ourselves whether we really want to know (vv. 1–4).

Seek wisdom

If we want wisdom, we must use every faculty in our search. The attentive ear, the receptive and lively mind, the voice which is not afraid to ask questions are all mentioned (vv. 1–3). But above all, it is the will to learn that drives us on towards discovery and growth.

Jesus tells a story about treasure hidden in a field. The man who finds it is ready to sacrifice everything he has, if only he can buy the field and own the treasure (Matthew 13:44). Here in Proverbs, Wisdom is just as valuable as that treasure. Are we prepared for an equally single-minded quest to find and keep her?

The search must be worth it, because when we persevere until we find and 'understand' (literally, learn discrimination) about loving reverence for God (v. 5) we discover that God's wisdom is free (vv. 5–7a). Knowledge and understanding come 'from his mouth', that is, directly from his presence. He has them stored up and waiting for us; he 'gives good things to those who ask him' (Matthew 7:11). We are not like the man who sold everything he had to buy the field with the hidden treasure. We do not have to pay any money to know God's ways; he only asks for our commitment.

What are the benefits of God's gift?

First, if we 'walk blamelessly'—that is, in integrity—our lifestyle, lived in obedience to God, will itself be our protection (v. 7b). We shall be his 'faithful ones', or 'special ones' (v. 8)—different from other people (not always popular with them and certainly not exempt from trouble and sorrow). But in our walk through life we can rely on the presence of the One who is 'a sun and shield' (Psalm 84:11).

Second, when we have made our commitment to God's ways, we shall understand that this joyful life will come about as a result of knowledge as well as behaviour (vv. 9–10). Then we shall become acquainted with righteousness (what is true and just), justice (how to make accurate moral decisions) and uprightness (how to live a life of integrity)—all subjects in the curriculum laid down in chapter 1 (see 1:3) and all leading us into good ways.

TO THINK ABOUT

Jesus says, 'Enter through the narrow gate; for the gate is wide and the road is easy that leads to destruction, and there are many who take it. For the gate is narrow and the road is hard that leads to life, and there are few who find it' (Matthew 7:13–14).

PRAYER

Lord, I do want to know your ways and walk in your paths. Please help me as I seek the wisdom that you promise, and then give me the strength and perseverance to live my life as you want me to, and to remember that you will never leave me.

BENEFITS & DANGERS

The teaching continues, but God is not mentioned; the emphasis is on the possession of wisdom—not a great change, since this wisdom is his wisdom. The consequences of what we think and do are spelt out in explicit detail.

Freedom to choose

We must choose to cultivate wisdom and knowledge, and 'prudence', or discretion; nobody can force them on us. However, they are worth the effort. Knowledge is 'pleasant' (v. 10)—literally, lovely, or delightful—not a usual thought, but one which points out the pleasure of a well-regulated life. Understanding and discretion will do the work of God himself (vv. 7–8) and give us protection.

At this point, the meaning of this protection is explained in some detail.

Protection from twisted values

'Perverse', 'crooked' and 'devious' all have an element of 'turning upside down'. We need to be on our guard against those who twist every word (v. 12), who prefer shady dealings to honesty (v. 13), and whose values call black white and white black (v. 14). However, the heart of this passage is in verses 16–19, which are about the need for protection against the temptress.

Wisdom's opposite

Here we are introduced to Wisdom's opposite number, who comes over in the first place as a real person rather than an abstract quality. The two words translated 'loose woman' and 'adulteress' are literally 'foreigner' and 'alien'; in this context they probably mean a 'stranger' —someone else's wife, who should have no place in the life of the foolish one who dallies with her (v. 16). She is plausible, and she is unfaithful to the partner whom she married in youth (v. 17). Proverbs takes a firm line about the seriousness and permanence of marriage, and is always outspoken on the subject. It is a sacred covenant— literally 'the covenant of (her) God'—not to be forgotten or set aside. To give in to temptation in this respect is compared with death in that there is no way back (the Babylonians referred to the afterlife as 'the land of no return') (vv. 18–19). This is harsh, but many will admit that after an episode involving unfaithfulness, even when everything has been forgiven, life is never the same again.

However, there may be a second, more spiritual meaning to these words. The writer could be thinking of the prophet Hosea who, though his wife Gomer was an adulteress, never stopped loving her, and took her back (Hosea 1—3). Hosea's story reflects God's faithful love for his people, who have broken their covenant with him, but who are still forgiven and restored to their former relationship with him.

So although we have to live with the consequences of our foolishness and indiscretion, nothing is unforgivable with God, who promises:

I will heal their disloyalty;
  I will love them freely (Hosea 14:4).

Pointing the moral

Therefore watch your step, walk obediently, and you will be secure (v. 20). To 'abide in the land' (v. 21) is in the Old Testament a sign of God's favour. Knowing that we are God's children—forgiven, healed and supported—brings with it the responsibility of living our lives in obedience to his commandments, and taking time to seek his guidance in the many difficult decisions we have to make. This means self-discipline, but it leads to peace and safety.

PRAYER
Almighty and everlasting Father...
Keep us from falling into sin
or running into danger;
order us in all our doings;
and guide us to do always
what is right in your eyes;
through Jesus Christ our Lord.

Collect for Morning Prayer, *Alternative Service Book 1980*

FATHERLY ADVICE (III)

These verses list the first three of six duties towards God and the rewards which come when we fulfil these duties: knowledge of the past and hope for the future; loyalty and good reputation; and trust and divine guidance.

Past knowledge and future hope

For spiritual life and growth, we need to know our spiritual heritage (vv. 1–2). Here, as throughout Judaism and indeed Proverbs itself, the need to teach the younger generation the faiths and truths of its history is emphasized. 'Remember' means 'remember what you have been told', for we can only begin to know God by first understanding something about how he has dealt with his people.

The reward for looking back and learning is having something to which we can look forward—a long life. To the Christian, whose 'citizenship is in heaven' (Philippians 3:20), this may not seem so important, but in Proverbs, as elsewhere in the Old Testament, the doctrine of the afterlife is not so well developed. So length of life and 'abundant welfare'—perhaps here meaning inner wholeness and outward serenity as much as material prosperity—are signs of God's approval.

Loyalty and reputation

'Loyalty' and 'faithfulness' (v. 3) go together twenty-three times in the Old Testament. 'Loyalty' is sometimes translated 'steadfast love', and 'faithfulness' is from the same root as 'Amen', meaning 'to confirm', or 'to support', and implies stability. Both words belong to the covenant relationship between God and his people and each word depends on the other. Loyalty prevents faithfulness from becoming harsh and legalistic; faithfulness prevents loyalty from degenerating into weak sentimentality. Once again there is an echo of Deuteronomy 6:8–9: 'Bind (these words) as a sign on your hand, fix them as an emblem on your forehead, and write them on the doorposts of your house and on your gates.' Love and loyalty to God are to be an essential part of daily life, symbolized later by the phylacteries and tephillim—tiny boxes containing quotations from the Law—which the Jews wore tied round their foreheads and left arms, and fastened to their doorposts.

The reward for steadfastness is a good reputation (v. 4); consistency is respected. 'Good repute' is related to 'wise dealing', and 'favour' directs our attention to the 'divine and human favour' into which Jesus grew (Luke 2:52).

Trust and divine guidance

Trusting God with all our hearts (literally, minds) (v. 5), rather than relying on our own insight, does not mean abdicating responsibility for making judgments. Nor does it mean that we shall be free from problems in deciding what is best. Rather, it involves a new approach —reversing our natural inclination to make our own plans first and then ask for God's endorsement of them and co-operation with them.

The promise 'He will make straight your paths' (v. 6; see also Isaiah 40:3) seems to suggest that if we trust in God he will smooth out the rough places in our lives. This is the language of faith rather than of experience; there are plenty of examples in Proverbs where life is anything but smooth. The point here is that we are encouraged to trust even when things are not very clear, confident that God knows the future and that his love provides our security.

TO THINK ABOUT

God holds the key of all unknown,
and I am glad;
If other hands should hold the key,
or if he trusted it to me,
I might be sad.
What if tomorrow's cares were here
without its rest!
I'd rather he unlocked the day;
and, as the hours swing open, say,
'My will is best'.

Joseph Parker (1830–1902)

7 PROVERBS 3:7–12

FATHERLY ADVICE (IV)

The list of duties towards God and their rewards, begun in the first part of the chapter, continues with the final three: humility and healing; generosity and provision; and love and discipline.

Humility and healing

True humility (vv. 7–8) means first, reverence for God and the acknowledgment that his ways are right. Then there is the matter of a right attitude to others: Paul writes, 'Do not be haughty, but associate with the lowly; do not claim to be wiser than you are' (Romans 12:16)—not always easy advice to follow.

The consequent 'healing' and 'refreshment' which are promised touch every part of us; 'flesh' is literally 'navel', 'body' literally 'bones' —that is, the centre of our being and our whole frame. In the Bible 'health' is holistic; to be 'whole' means being right with God at every level. However, this does not necessarily include perfect physical fitness; again, there is plenty in Proverbs about illness and depression. Rather, it is a reminder that spiritual, physical and emotional health are bound up with each other, and that to be in a right relationship with God and with other people is essential to well-being. There is nothing new about psychosomatic illness!

Generosity and provision

Giving back to God 'some of the first of all the fruit of the ground', in acknowledgment that the harvest was his gift, was originally an agricultural practice (Deuteronomy 26:2, 10) and this is a rare reference in Proverbs (usually more interested in practical matters) to anything ceremonial. Its inclusion (vv. 9–10) suggests that there is an important principle here. What we have is given to us by God, and we must seek his guidance in the matter of giving. However, 'honouring the Lord with our substance' is not an easy method of ensuring that God will make us richer still. It is an acknowledgment that everything we have is his gift.

Some commentators remark that the promise (v. 10) about 'barns' and 'vats' refers only to the staples of life, bread and wine, which can be shared with the needy. It does not present a prospect of ever-increasing luxury.

Love and discipline

After all the glowing promises, we come to the reality that no life is trouble-free (vv. 11–12). These verses give an early warning that the looked-for prosperity does not always translate into painless experience. Sadness, failure, discouragement, illness and all sorts of other difficulties are common to us all. What are we to make of our disappointments?

The biblical writers, especially Wisdom writers, wrestle with the problem of suffering, and with the deeply held belief that it is in some way a punishment for sin—a doctrine which the New Testament makes clear is not a true interpretation of the experience. Seeing a man blind from birth, Jesus' disciples asked, 'Rabbi, who sinned, this man or his parents, that he was born blind?' Jesus answered, 'Neither this man nor his parents sinned; he was born blind so that God's works might be revealed in him' (John 9:2–3).

Here in Proverbs the writer, who has not seen the works of Jesus, cannot have such an advanced doctrine. However, he makes his own contribution to the ongoing debate. This is the only place in the book where God is compared to a father, and the words are not punishment but discipline; not retribution but reproof. There is a disciplinary element in God's love and care. Job, in the middle of dreadful trouble, says, 'How happy is the one whom God reproves; therefore do not despise the discipline of the Almighty' (Job 5:17). But there is an even deeper meaning for us to think about. Verses 11 and 12 are quoted in Hebrews 12:5–6, introducing teaching about being children of God. Suffering is not only to be accepted as children must accept discipline; it links us with the One who 'although he was a Son, learned obedience through what he suffered' (Hebrews 5:8).

PRAYER

Almighty God, who alone can bring order to the unruly wills and passions of sinful humanity: give your people grace so to love what you command and to desire what you promise, that in all the changes and chances of this world, our hearts may surely there be fixed where true joys are to be found; through Jesus Christ your Son our Lord.

Collect for the 3rd Sunday before Lent, *Common Worship*

8 PROVERBS 3:13–20

WISDOM'S PORTRAIT (II)

This time it is not Wisdom who speaks but the author, who adds to the portrait begun in Proverbs 1:20–33. What do we learn that is new?

Wisdom is a source of happiness

The first and last word of verses 13–18 is 'happy'. What sort of happiness does Wisdom bring? With one exception (16:20) 'happy' is used in Proverbs of individual rather than national, and moral rather than spiritual, well-being. Wisdom offers happiness in several ways.

She offers us gifts

The picture of Wisdom standing holding gifts (v. 16) has something in common with the way the Egyptian Maat, the goddess of truth and order, is represented. We are already familiar with the promised benefits of long life, riches and honour. Perhaps 'long life', because it is held in her right hand, is even more precious than 'riches and honour'.

She offers us direction

'Her ways are ways of pleasantness and all her paths are peace' (v. 17) is not simply a promise of comfort and the absence of hostilities; it means good relationships between people, and between ourselves and God. It promises serenity in our inner hearts and outward dealings, and reminds us of Psalm 23:2:

He makes me lie down in green pastures;
he leads me beside still waters.

She offers us a life of quality

Wisdom is not only a life-enhancer; she is a life-giver (v. 18), likened to the 'tree of life'. This tree appears elsewhere in the Bible, from Genesis 2:9, where it is planted together with the other (forbidden) tree from which the man and the woman ate fruit, to Revelation 22:2, where it is fruitful and its leaves are 'for the healing of the nations'.

The first man and woman were banished from the tree of life, but its blessings of peace, wholeness and contentment are still on offer to those who find God's Wisdom, and who persevere in treasuring her. This is the condition on which happiness depends; it is not automatic: 'Those who hold her fast are called happy.'

Wisdom is infinitely precious

We have already been told that Wisdom is a great treasure to be sought after (2:4–5). Here her value is emphasized. She is more profitable than monetary wealth (v. 14), and she is beautiful as well as valuable (v. 15). 'Jewels' can mean literally 'something red' and may refer to rubies, or to coral, which was much prized in the ancient world. Wisdom is to be treasured as we treasure what is most dear to us.

Verses 19 and 20 move from ourselves receiving good things, to Wisdom herself, presenting her as the Wisdom of God the Creator.

God's tool

The focus shifts from Wisdom to God; she was his tool in creation. The idea of the earth in verse 20 was usual in the author's time: a flat disc, with the subterranean waters gushing upwards as seas, springs and rivers, and with moisture dropping from the vault of the sky. Wisdom was not only present at a past event; she is part of the continuing direction of the physical world, for example in the distribution of water.

So all life comes to us and is sustained in and around us through the power and love of God—both human life and life in the world of nature. This calls not only for wonder and gratitude, but also for responsible stewardship of the whole of God's creation. Later this is spelt out in practical terms, and Wisdom's creativity is described vividly. The message here is that the way of Wisdom is to live in harmony with God's created order.

TO THINK ABOUT

If God, with Wisdom as his tool, created and maintains the world, what will he create in our lives if we find and cherish Wisdom?

FATHERLY ADVICE (V)

After the exalted picture of Wisdom in verses 19 and 20, we have some down-to-earth, practical teaching. Verses 27–31 are the central part of the chapter, and probably the oldest, because they are written in the same style as the other pieces of 'fatherly advice'. However, the introduction and epilogue, though likely to have been added later, because they introduce a spiritual element missing from the 'central' verses, give helpful and relevant advice.

A life of security

This is the theme of verses 21–26. Our part is never to lose sight of the wisdom and knowledge of verses 19 and 20 nor of the prudence involved in preserving sound judgment (v. 21) but to hold them fast. The result will be 'life for your soul'—a source of vitality—and 'adornment (literally "a charm") for your neck', meaning perhaps protection, or alternatively the gracious demeanour which comes from inner confidence.

This confidence brings freedom from fear, one of God's greatest blessings, given to us when we are guided by his divine wisdom. It enhances our lives both outside and inside our homes, and it keeps us from panic when disaster strikes those who are not living in harmony with God's will.

The idea of life as a journey on which the traveller needs divine protection is frequent in the Psalms as well as Proverbs: 'stumble' in verse 23 is the same word as 'dash your foot' (against a stone) in Psalm 91:12. Similarly, the reminder of God's presence in our family lives, in verse 24, yet again echoes 'when you are home and when you are away, when you lie down and when you rise' in Deuteronomy 6:7, and 'I lie down and sleep; I wake again, for the Lord sustains me' in Psalm 3:5. These promises are not made in isolation; they are in tune with the rest of the Old Testament.

Warnings against anti-social behaviour

These occupy verses 27–31. The central principle is generosity; to exercise it involves avoiding meanness, needless delay in doing good, malicious conspiracy, contentiousness and inappropriate envy.

'From those to whom it is due' (v. 27) can be translated 'from the needy', so we can read this as urging us to show liberality and kindness as well as honesty in paying debts. All wages, debts and help in general must be paid or given promptly (v. 28). As James 2:16 asks, 'If a brother or sister is naked and lacks daily food, and one of you says to them, "Go in peace; keep warm and eat your fill", and yet you do not supply their bodily needs, what is the good of that?'

The warnings against conspiring to do harm, particularly where the object of our plotting has no idea that anything is the matter, and picking a quarrel (not necessarily litigation, but any needless dispute, vv. 29–30) show a realistic view of the difficulties of living in a community. However, it is envy of the 'violent' (v. 31) that is often our greatest problem. It would be easy to say, 'Accept that crime does not pay', but this is not borne out by what we see. 'Violent' can refer to anyone who is unscrupulous or high-handed, and the outcome of their conduct is often financial gain. Psalm 73 deals at length with this particular manifestation of the unfairness of life, and finds no easy solution, except in the knowledge that all worldly success is at best short-lived and ultimately unsatisfactory (Psalm 73:19–20), and that God's presence in our lives is the most important and satisfying thing to possess (Psalm 73:28). In fact, as Proverbs 3:32 points out, there are no real grounds for envy of such people; they are displeasing to God, and in the long run will be disgraced, while those of integrity are God's familiar friends—'confidence' here means 'intimate, private conversation'.

Epilogue

Verses 32–35 contrast wisdom and folly, arrogance and humility, God's blessing and God's curse. Verse 34, in slightly different form, is quoted in James 4:6 and in 1 Peter 5:6. The special grace promised to those who seek humility, and its eventual triumph, are an important part of Christian teaching from the earliest times.

PRAYER ✗

Lord, your standards are very high, and I am often selfish and demanding, and proud and jealous. Please give me the grace you have promised to overcome these faults and to live at peace with others and in harmony with you. Thank you because I have a special friendship with you when I walk in your ways.

10   PROVERBS 4:1–9

FATHERLY ADVICE (VI)

The influence of the home

This, the first of three 'parental talks' in this chapter, each pointing to some aspect of Wisdom's excellence, is something new, because instead of giving practical advice it reminisces about the father's own childhood.

It begins in the usual way, with admonitions that are similar to 1:2; 'instruction' and 'insight', with their undertones of discipline and understanding, both appear there. The father has confidence in his teaching, since it is grounded in his own experience. The 'precepts' which he shares with others are the 'learning' which is received by others in 1:5.

He looks back and gives a vivid picture of the loving home in which he was brought up, when he was 'tender'—meaning young in years—and his mother's 'only one', or 'only beloved'. The NRSV interprets the phrase as 'his mother's favourite'; the RSV has 'the only one in the sight of his mother'. It was here that he received his first teaching, and it would have been oral; books were rare and in the main for use only by advanced students, although the children of more prosperous families would be taught to read. He implies that he was a receptive pupil; what he learned has stayed with him, and he is eager to pass it on to the next generation. Inevitably we are shaped by our parents; inevitably we shape the next generation. Here, the father has a good tradition to pass on; less fortunate parents have to make a conscious effort to break the 'cycle of deprivation' and try to instil good habits and godly ways. There is no better place for a child to learn by precept and by example than in the home; there is no better time than in early life.

The teaching in the home

Verses 4–9 have been called 'an address within an address', passing on what was taught to the writer. It begins as we might expect, with an exhortation to get and retain wisdom and insight (v. 5), and to 'keep my commandments and live'—though whether this refers to length of life or quality of life is not clear.

In verse 6 the train of thought passes from familiar ideas born of experience to the praise of Wisdom and the concept of love. In the Law, love is for God and others (Deuteronomy 6:4; Leviticus 19:18); in the Prophets it is for right conduct (Amos 5:15; Micah 3:2); in the Psalms, for God's Law and for Zion, his dwelling-place (Psalm 26:8; 119:97). The command here is to love Wisdom—who becomes a person rather than an abstract quality, and in the following verses 'getting Wisdom' is described as we might describe seeking and finding a wife.

Verse 7 is not easy to fit in with the thoughts in verses 6 and 8, both of which are very specific about aspects of our relationship with Wisdom. It is not included in the Greek Old Testament and possibly it was originally a note in the margin, summarizing verses 4–9, which then became part of the main text.

The last two verses continue the theme of courtship and marriage. We are to prize and protect Wisdom highly (literally, 'to cast up an embankment', and so to 'raise up'), and to embrace her (literally 'fold her in our arms'). In return, she will exalt those who prize her, honour those who love her wholeheartedly, and bring grace to their lives. The 'beautiful crown' (v. 9) is probably a reference to the custom of wearing crowns or garlands at weddings and other joyful occasions. To find, keep and cherish Wisdom is a matter for thanksgiving.

TO THINK ABOUT

'I will walk with integrity of heart within my house' (Psalm 101:2). How far is this true of me in my relationships in the home? Is my home life consistent with my public life?

PRAYER

Lord, I need your help in the home. Help me to be patient and loving, yet firm and clear in what I convey to my family by word and example. Give me your guidance about when to speak and when to keep silence; when to act and when to stay still. I entrust all my loved ones to your unfailing love, knowing that you can work where I am helpless.

FATHERLY ADVICE (VII)

The two ways

The theme of two ways is an ancient one, used by the early Egyptian teacher Ptah-hotep. It has been a favourite way of expressing moral and spiritual teaching in both Judaism and Christianity; it appears in the Sermon on the Mount (Matthew 7:13–14). In these verses, walking, running, stumbling, turning away and passing on are all used to describe following a path, or a chosen way of living, with its characteristic behaviour and attitudes.

The writer begins with his usual plea to take notice, with the promised reward of long life, and then strongly recommends the way of Wisdom.

The well-made road

Wisdom's way (vv. 10–13) is like a well-made, well-defined road. Following it means obeying the teaching of Wisdom, and committing yourself to an upright lifestyle. It seems strange that 'stumble' in verse 12 comes from a word meaning 'to be narrow', and indicates distress and unhappiness. So 'If you run, you will not stumble' means 'True happiness is yours when you walk wisely'.

The father places great stress on this teaching; he strongly encourages his offspring to develop the style and character that will lead to life, whether of good length or of good quality (v. 13; see also v. 4).

The way of wickedness

This is in stark contrast. 'Do not enter… do not walk… avoid… turn away and pass on from' this path is the fourfold instruction in verses 14 and 15. Travellers along this road are corrupt and violent, with the violence which means unkindness, oppression, robbery and murder. Their purpose in living is to do wrong and to incite others to join them. They cannot sleep unless they have indulged in these activities—a reversal of the usual pattern where a bad conscience prevents sleep (v. 16). Their wicked ways are food and drink to them—essential to life itself (v. 17). This picture may owe something to life in the great cities of the period—the historian Josephus writes of unscrupulous, grasping and desperate characters who roamed the streets and were a danger to society.

Is the contrast between good and evil too simplistic here? It certainly goes against the modern tendency to recognize both good and bad in everything and everyone. Or is there something to be said for the view that evil, whatever its degree, is always evil, and is to be rejected at all times?

The essential difference between these two ways is summed up in verses 18 and 19. One is dark (v. 19), with the deep, unchanging darkness which obscures the intellect and destroys any sense of direction. The other is clear and light (v. 18), with a brightness that grows from the first light of dawn to the full sunlight of noon. Because of Wisdom's origin, those who follow her way will have the light of God's guidance, which continually increases and gives safety and security.

TO THINK ABOUT

The options are set out clearly, and there is a free choice to be made, which is not always as simple as these verses describe. How can we know what is right? Read Psalm 27:11–14. Pray the prayer for guidance found there, then ask that you will be able to 'be strong, and let your heart take courage', and receive the promise that at the end of the journey you will 'see the goodness of the Lord in the land of the living'.

FATHERLY ADVICE (VIII)

Be vigilant

The introduction (vv. 20–22) emphasizes the importance of holding fast to the words of instruction, and claims that they bring healing, or well-being, to the flesh, or body—meaning our whole being.

This is a starting-point for the key words in this discourse—heart, speech, eyes and feet. We need to be watchful over every part of ourselves.

First, the heart, or mind. When we talk about 'being ruled by our heart, not our head', we mean being ruled by our feelings rather than by our intelligence. But in the Old Testament, 'keep your heart' (v. 23) means the opposite—'Be ruled by your intelligence rather than by your emotions.' The 'heart' is the seat not of feelings but of intelligence and will; it controls how we think and act; it is our real self, known only to God. 'For the Lord does not see as mortals see; they look on the outward appearance, but the Lord looks on the heart' (1 Samuel 16:7). If our heart is right with God, this will be reflected in our conduct:

> I treasure your word in my heart,
> so that I may not sin against you (Psalm 119:11).

Elsewhere in Proverbs, life flows from Wisdom and obedience to instruction, not from the heart, so 'from it (the heart) flow the springs of life' (v. 23) probably means that life springs from our vigilance and control.

The mouth (or speech) is understood to be identical with our thoughts (v. 24). The trouble starts when it is not—when it becomes 'crooked' and 'devious' and when one untruth spoken by us is distorted by further untruths. Thoughts once put into words acquire a life of their own beyond our control, so we do well to be on our guard about what we say. Discretion was part of the training of court officials over all the ancient Near East; the Babylonian 'Counsels of Wisdom' commands, 'Let your mouth be controlled and your speech guarded'; and an early Egyptian document says, 'Guard your mouth more carefully than anything else.' The power of words is taken up in the New Testament in the letter of James: James 3:3–12 develops the theme that 'the tongue is a small member, yet it boasts of great exploits' (James 3:5).

Next comes the guardianship of our eyes (v. 25)—to this day a part of Christian moral theology. Eyes that 'look directly forward' are taken as evidence of an honest mind; 'to look someone straight in the eye' expresses the same idea. This also implies that we should not contemplate certain things. 'Turn my eyes from looking at vanities' (Psalm 119:37) should be used as a prayer not that we may go though life blind to what is happening, but that we may take care not to dwell on what is unhelpful, inappropriate and downright evil. With so much of our present culture geared to the visual, this is a timely warning.

'Watch your step' (v. 26) follows up the teaching in verses 10–19 about the two ways. 'Keep straight' means 'make a clear, firm road through life'. The same words can refer to the preparation of a highway for a king or an army—hills and valleys levelled, crooked and treacherous places smoothed (Isaiah 40:3–4). Organizing our lives so that we walk the way of Wisdom and not the way of wickedness takes determination and courage, but leads to stability.

TO THINK ABOUT

This vigilance is presented as our own responsibility. How can we manage it? Is there any help? Look at Psalm 121 and think about the promises which God makes.

PRAYER

Almighty God,
you see that we have no power of ourselves to help ourselves.
Keep us both outwardly in our bodies
and inwardly in our souls,
that we may be defended from all adversities
which may happen to the body,
and from all evil thoughts
which may assault and hurt the soul;
through Jesus Christ our Lord.

Post-Communion Prayer for the 2nd Sunday of Lent,
Common Worship

13 PROVERBS 5:1–14

FATHERLY ADVICE (IX)

Warnings and regrets

This is the second of six passages in chapters 1—9 which deal with avoiding adultery (the first is 2:16–19). Commentators differ, but the general feeling is that these verses are addressed to a young, unmarried man who is attracted to an unscrupulous married woman, and their severely practical tone suggests that this time they are to be taken at their face value rather than being read as a warning against idolatry (see the connection with Hosea suggested on page 25).

Why, we may ask, is there nothing about the danger to women of seduction by men? The answer probably lies in the social arrangements of the time, when women were fairly closely guarded, and in the corresponding failure to grant moral independence to women, as has always been reflected in works on practical ethics. The only Old Testament passages which directly address women concern their lifestyle (Isaiah 3:16—4:1; Amos 4:1–3) and some of the activities of prophetesses (Ezekiel 13:17–23).

Keep clear of the temptress

This is the advice in verses 1–10. The 'loose' or 'alien' woman's charms are alluring (v. 3). She is smooth and pleasant; her lips 'drip honey' and her speech (literally her palate, the seat of physical taste, intellectual discernment and its expression in words) is almost cloying in its sweetness.

In stark contrast is what happens to those who believe her—the words are 'wormwood', 'sharp', 'death'. Her real nature is 'bitter as wormwood'—the plant *artemesia absinthe*, used in the Old Testament as a symbol of suffering. The smooth talking conceals a cutting, destructive nature. The crooked, unstable path she walks leads to the loss of honour and wealth (the 'strangers' and 'alien' of verse 10 may mean pitiless creditors or even the woman's own husband). Finally comes a premature and unhappy death (v. 11; see also 2:18 and 4:19). It is not surprising that the seriousness of the warning is emphasized in verse 8.

'If only'

Vain regrets come later (vv. 11–14). The end of it all is the destruction of the 'flesh and body', that is, the whole personality. The worst damage is not so much the physical consequences of excess, painful though these may be, but the failure of all that makes life enjoyable. The victim has been brought to the 'point of utter ruin' (v. 14). The 'public assembly' is the official gathering of the community to consider breaches of the law; this offender comes near to suffering the ultimate punishment of death.

'If only' sums up verses 12 and 13. All the warning voices echo in the memory. Obedience to and respect for mature advice would have saved the young man from his unhappy fate. This is an extreme case, but remorse of this kind is common to many of us as we look back in later life to those who tried to guide us when we were young.

TO THINK ABOUT

The psalmist writes of the Children of Israel:

Some sat in darkness and in gloom,
prisoners in misery and in irons,
for they had rebelled against the words of God,
and spurned the counsel of the Most High....
Then they cried to the Lord in their trouble,
and he saved them from their distress.
(Psalm 107:10–11, 13)

PRAYER

Lord, help me to understand that remorse by itself can be destructive. I pray that you will 'save me from my distress' as you did your people long ago.

FAITHFULNESS *in* MARRIAGE

It is the turn of the older, married man to be given advice and warnings. This passage starts from the assumption that most men are married (as was the custom of the time), that infidelity is all too common, and that faithfulness is non-negotiable.

'Faithfulness brings happiness' is the theme of verses 15–20. Marriage is described first in picture language (vv. 15–17). In Isaiah 36:16, to 'drink water from your own cistern' describes the enjoyment of your own home; in Song of Solomon 4:15, the beloved is 'a garden fountain, a well of living water'. The cistern and the well are attached to the house; 'springs' and 'streams' are outside it. Why, asks the writer, seek your pleasure in the streets—the prostitute's territory? Why share it with others rather than enjoying it with your wife? (vv. 16–17).

Intoxicating love

In verses 18–20 the advice is explicit. The 'wife of your youth' (which can mean either 'your young wife' or 'the one whom you married in youth') remains beautiful and desirable, and her husband must be 'intoxicated' (literally 'infatuated') by her love. Among ancient peoples, marriage was regarded as a duty, and early marriage was the general custom, probably as a safeguard against promiscuity. But here, love is a matter of will and perseverance as well as of inclination, as our marriage service recognizes when it asks, 'Will you... forsaking all others, be faithful to him/her as long as you both shall live?'

All this deals only with the physical and emotional aspect of marriage; the wife is not described as a mother or as an intellectual companion. However, it is not the whole picture: Proverbs 31:10–31 presents a much broader view of this ideal, loving and lasting relationship.

That there are sometimes great difficulties in achieving and keeping to this high standard, which involves feelings as well as actions, is acknowledged in verse 20, which injects a note of harsh realism into the idyllic picture of the previous verses. Later Jewish teaching, perhaps aware that these instructions might be rejected as too difficult, interprets the wife as the Law, and adds, 'Wisdom learn

thou always, and to the love of it even more strongly apply thyself.'
However, the majority opinion about this passage is that it is to be
taken literally and its demands seriously.

Taking care

The conclusion (vv. 21–23) gives a reason for taking care in our
conduct—the knowledge that God knows and is concerned with
every detail of our lives. When that care is not taken, the wrongdoer
becomes entangled in his own misdemeanours, like an animal caught
in a net. But unlike the animal, he is responsible for his predicament;
he has not been subject to discipline in the sense of 'instruction' in
1:3. So this again ends in the disaster of a life which has taken no
heed of Wisdom.

PRAYER

*Lord, give me your faithful and steadfast love in every aspect of my
life. Help me to be loving even when I do not feel loving. Give me
the grace and strength to work at all my relationships, and to see
your image in others.*

15 PROVERBS 6:1–11

SOME PRACTICAL ADVICE

Although these verses begin, 'My child', they do not conform to the usual pattern of a direction to hear or be attentive, followed by praise of Wisdom. It is even possible that 'my child' is a later addition, so 6:1–19 is not as a rule included in the collection of 'fatherly talks'. Verses 1–19 divide into four sections, each dealing with a specific situation or condition which we should avoid.

Reckless generosity

The first piece of advice is, 'Do not make rash promises'. The particular example (vv. 1–5) is taken from the world of business. We see someone in debt, and guarantee to repay their loan if they cannot do so. It could be a friend, or even a 'stranger', as 'another' in verse 1 can be translated—it may have been difficult to set up in business without being vouched for by an Israelite. The Law encourages help for those in need, provided no interest is charged (Exodus 22:25); but in this case a moment of reckless generosity has presumably led to a commitment which it will be difficult to meet, and we are caught in a trap of our own making.

The remedy is to face up to the situation, and swallow our pride ('hurry' in verse 3 can also mean 'humble yourself'). Then we must take urgent action (v. 4) to disentangle ourselves from the situation. 'Plead' (v. 3) is a strong word—it means literally to besiege someone. At whatever cost to our self-esteem, we must extricate ourselves from this entanglement which has put us into someone else's power (v. 3). Loss of face must not be a consideration.

We can also take this warning in a general sense. Do not make thoughtless, impulsive commitments. Think hard before promising anything, and if you do make a mistake, admit it at once. This is the only way to manage our relationships with honesty and integrity.

Industry and sloth

A warning against laziness follows (vv. 6–11). It is a parable addressed to the 'lazybones', a word used only in Proverbs. The industry of the ant is held up as an example of how to avoid poverty and want. Learning from nature is mentioned later in Proverbs (30:24–31) and elsewhere in the Old Testament Wisdom literature—for example:

Ask the animals, and they will teach you;
the birds of the air, and they will tell you;
ask the plants of the earth and they will teach you;
and the fish of the sea will declare to you (Job 12:7–8).

We now know that the ant has a highly intricate and even regimented pattern of life, but the writer, observing how it organizes its time, finds it all the more commendable because it works, he believes, without oversight from line-manager, police or local executive (v. 7). It is diligent, thrifty and far-sighted (v. 8).

The opposite of this is sloth. 'A little... a little... a little...' may be the continuation of the warning, or the lazybones' irritated response to admonition. In either case, laziness, which means the abandonment of responsibility, results in poverty—a state of deprivation which is like a powerful and ruthless enemy, carrying off suddenly and even violently all that the sluggard holds dear. The picture is of it happening unexpectedly, without warning and without reprieve.

TO THINK ABOUT

Impetuosity and laziness are two opposite faults. We are likely to
be more inclined to one than to the other, but we need to guard
against both, prayerfully to admit our weaknesses whatever they
are, and be prepared to take action to correct them.

PRAYER

Who can detect their errors?
Clear me from hidden faults.
Keep back your servant also from proud thoughts;
do not let them have dominion over me.
Then I shall be blameless,
and innocent of great transgression.
(Psalm 19:12–13)

AVOID MISCHIEF-MAKING

The next warning is about a bad role model (vv. 12–15). There is so much about the habitual mischief-maker in Proverbs and in non-Israelite wisdom literature that we must conclude that he was one of the main curses of ancient Near Eastern society—as he is of any society. He is not a pleasant person to know, and the sharp, terse tone of verses 12–15 reflects the writer's distaste. He is a scoundrel (literally, a worthless person), and totally depraved. Predictably, his words are twisted, and he spreads them around, causing the maximum amount of damage (v. 12).

In verse 13 the three bodily gestures, winking, shuffling and pointing or 'teaching' with the fingers, convey a vivid impression of malicious hints, suggestions and signals which aim to provoke a quarrel. It has even been suggested that in making these signs to his fellow conspirators the villain is employing magical means to achieve his purpose. The use of hostile body language is not peculiar to Proverbs. Job 16:9–10 reads:

> He has gnashed his teeth at me,
>   my adversary sharpens his eyes against me.
> They have gaped at me with their mouths;
>   they have struck me insolently on the cheek;
>   they mass themselves together against me.

The end comes with devastating suddenness, and is again described in abrupt, vehement terms (v. 15). The 'damage beyond repair' must refer to death, for there is no way back from Sheol, and no chance of this man improving his standing and gaining favour with God.

Seven things to avoid

The numerical pattern 'x... and x+1' (v. 16) appears not only elsewhere in the Bible—(see Proverbs 30:18, 21, 29; Amos 1:3—2:8, 'for three transgressions... and for four')—but in writings from Egypt and Mesopotamia. Ahikar, an Assyrian sage writing in mid-seventh century BC, has:

There are two things that are excellent
and three that give pleasure to (the god) Shamash.

The formula may represent the classifying of natural phenomena as a stage in the search for a fuller understanding of the world; it may be a device to direct our attention to the last saying in the group; or it may simply be the equivalent of our 'six or seven'—an indefinite expression. Whichever it is, the message is clear. Certain things are totally unacceptable to God, so we must shun them. Once again, our bodies can reveal our thoughts and intentions. 'Haughtiness', which implies not only excessive conceit and self-regard but disregard for the rights of others, is naturally expressed by our looks. The tongue speaks lies, sometimes to the extent of perjury (vv. 17, 19). 'Wicked plans' come from the heart and are not always detected by others; when they are carried out, the perpetrator's feet may rush eagerly to do harm (v. 18). Last, perhaps because most serious, comes stirring up dissension in the family or the community. Mischief-making is not to be regarded lightly; it is just as blameworthy as murder or lying.

TO THINK ABOUT

This passage makes depressing reading. What is pleasing to God,
and how can we achieve it? Paul writes:

'I appeal to you, therefore, brothers and sisters, by the mercies
of God, to present your bodies as a living sacrifice, holy and
acceptable to God, which is your spiritual worship. Do not be
conformed to this world, but be transformed by the renewing of
your minds, so that you may discern what is the will of God—
what is good and acceptable and perfect.'
(Romans 12:1–2)

FATHERLY ADVICE (X)

A third warning against adultery

At first sight this long passage may seem to cover familiar ground. There is the father's exhortation to the son to pay attention to his parents' teaching, the reminder of the benefits of obedience, the caution against adultery, and the description of its consequence. What is there here that we do not find in 2:16–19 and in chapter 5?

The answer is, several things: these verses build on, rather than repeat, what has already been said.

Wisdom saves

First, parental instruction is by implication identified with Wisdom. In 2:16 and 5:1 it is Wisdom, not teaching, that saves the young man from the adulteress. But here, in verse 22, 'they', apparently referring to the father's precepts, provide the necessary defence. However, 'they' translates the Hebrew word for 'she'—and surely 'she' must be Wisdom. The assumption is that in a well-ordered household the advice of the father and mother will be wise. So it is Wisdom who will watch over the son, talk with him, lead him in his active life, protect him when he lies helpless in sleep, and be there to give advice when he wakes. This guiding force is described as a light (v. 23), applied in Psalm 119:105 to God's word, and in later Judaism to Wisdom herself.

Costly adultery

Second, a distinction is made between the prostitute who will take her price from her client but will not ruin him and the seductive, plausible, smooth-talking 'wife of another', or 'evil woman' (v. 24) who will certainly take his reputation and may even take his life. This is not to say that the activities of a prostitute are less serious than those of an adulteress, but they can be less costly. The Revised English Bible has 'is after the prize of a life' instead of 'stalks a man's very life' (v. 26), which makes the meaning clearer.

Third, there is a special warning about sleeping with the wife of a 'neighbour'—presumably someone known to the offender (vv.

27–29). It is as dangerous and foolish as tipping burning wood into one's lap or walking on hot coals. No one can play with fire and expect to avoid the painful consequences. The law is so strict, or perhaps the wronged husband so determined, that no excuse which might be offered—for example, that of the encouragement given by the woman (v. 24)—will be accepted.

Fourth, there is another comparison, this time between the thief who steals to satisfy his hunger and the man who commits adultery (vv. 30–35). Here again, theft is not condoned; in the Old Testament a thief is thoroughly 'shamed' (Jeremiah 2:26). Nor need we feel sorry for this particular offender, because verse 31 shows him to be a man of property. All the same, he can atone for his sin by paying a heavy fine, but the adulterer, who lacks intelligence in getting himself into such difficulties (v. 32), is for ever disgraced and cannot buy his way out of trouble.

Finally, the woman's husband comes into the picture. Wild with jealousy and totally implacable, he will not be bought off, but will see to it that retribution comes. Under the Law of Moses the penalty for adultery was death for both parties (Leviticus 20:10, Deuteronomy 22:22); possibly this rigour was relaxed later, but there is no escaping punishment in this case. If the 'wounds and dishonour' of verse 33 are not the outcome of the legal process, they may come from the husband literally beating up his wife's lover. Either way, there is indelible disgrace.

Notice that all this concerns the man in the affair. No mention is made of any consequences for the woman; she is treated as her husband's property, and, we assume, his responsibility. This is a harsh passage, with no trace of the reconciliation in Hosea (see 2:16) or the mercy shown by Jesus (John 8:1–11); it is concerned to make clear the fearful consequences of living by foolish self-indulgence instead of in the light of divine wisdom.

TO THINK ABOUT

'For the commandment is a lamp and the teaching a light, and the reproofs of discipline are the way of life' (v. 23).

PRAYER

Lord, help me to walk in the light of your ways, and give me the grace to accept it when you correct me.

FATHERLY ADVICE (XI)

Chapter 7 begins and ends with the usual words of admonition and warning. In the middle (vv. 6–23) is a long and detailed poem, thought by some commentators to be an insertion because it reads like a personal story rather than a piece of advice, describing in detail the now-familiar figure of the adulteress, and the way she traps a young man.

Home truths

A desirable relationship for his young son is the father's urgent wish (vv. 1–5). Once again, his teachings are put side by side with Wisdom. They should be precious—'the apple of your eye' (v. 2) means the centre, or the pupil. Sometimes it is translated as 'the little man of the eye'—meaning the miniature reflection that we supposedly see if we look into someone's eyes. In either case, it means the most important and delicate part of the eye. The psalmist prays, 'Guard me as the apple of the eye' (Psalm 17:8).

Ideally, the home's teaching should always be kept in mind; the hands are usually in sight, so the fingers will be a constant reminder of what is engraved on the heart and the thoughts (v. 3).

But above all, like most responsible parents, the father wants the young man to live—long and happily. So how can the son be protected from the disillusionment, disappointment and destructiveness which come from an undesirable association? His parents, we can assume, believe that sexual commitment should be the expression of a stable, permanent, faithful relationship, and that to give yourself physically without emotional and spiritual commitment is to live a lie—to let your body say what your heart does not mean. Paul has the same thought in 1 Corinthians 6:16, when he says that no one can enjoy a relationship with a prostitute without some effect on the emotional and spiritual health.

This outlook was probably no more popular then than it is now, but the way forward chosen here is to draw clear boundaries, and to point to the path of safety and happiness. Wisdom, God's rule of life, must be regarded not as a tiresome duty, but as a loved relative (some translations read 'bride' for 'sister' in verse 4) and as a close friend.

Such an alliance, of course, brings obligations as well as pleasure; 'intimate friend' appears in Ruth 2:1 as 'kinsman'. So there is a discipline about making friends with Wisdom and putting her teaching first. It gives protection from the adulteress's wiles (v. 5), but it also means doing our part by determining to resist temptation. Wisdom does not do for us what we can do for ourselves.

On the street corner

A view from the window comes to deepen these anxieties (vv. 6–10). The scene is vividly described. Anyone standing inside the wooden or metal trellis-work of the unglazed window of an oriental house can see without being seen. Outside, the young and the 'simple' or easily led (see 1:4) are hanging about as they always have done. One of them, who, like the adulterer in 6:32, is conspicuously short on intelligence, strolls along the street near to the corner where the no-doubt notorious woman lives. He is putting himself in the way of danger— perhaps through bravado, perhaps through stupidity, perhaps through desire. The scene is the more sinister because it happens in the darkness—any time from twilight to the middle (the 'pupil') of the night—when those who walk the streets are often up to no good. How effective will the early teaching of a godly home now be in restraining this foolish youth?

TO THINK ABOUT

Paul writes to Timothy, 'I am reminded of your sincere faith, a faith that lived first in your grandmother Lois and your mother Eunice and now, I am sure, lives in you' (2 Timothy 1:5). We may not feel this confidence about our children, but often it is the early lessons that are remembered in much later life.

PORTRAIT *of a* TEMPTRESS

The poem turns from the hunted to the huntress.

Her dress is that of a prostitute—traditionally a veil (see Genesis 38:14), although in fact this is a deception, because she is a married woman. So she is from the start an imposter (v. 10).

Her manner is noisy and boisterous (v. 11)—the same word is used of the 'uproar' in Jerusalem in 1 Kings 1:41, when Solomon is anointed king and his rivals hear the shouting and the music, much to their dismay.

Her behaviour in public is self-willed and rebellious—careless of her duties to her home and her husband. She is free to wander about the city at night (v. 11). Earlier, the Law forbade women other than slaves to leave their homes after sunset, but by this time the rule seems to have been relaxed. In Song of Solomon 3:2–3 the heroine goes about the city with the watchmen, looking for her beloved.

All this is what immoral women of the time do—showing themselves freely in the streets and squares, and especially at corners—particularly convenient as places from which to see and be seen. It is a vivid description of city manners in the later Old Testament period.

A deceptive invitation

Her invitation is both brazen ('with impudent face', v. 13) and plausible. She has been making an offering in fulfilment of a vow or vows (such duties tend to pile up!) A sacrifice of meat must be made, and unlike the burnt offering, or 'holocaust', which is reduced to cinders on the altar, it is only partly destroyed. The rest is left for worshippers to eat with their families, and it has to be consumed on the same day (Leviticus 7:16). This is the sort of a festive occasion which, when it is celebrated in the wrong spirit, God detests:

> *I hate, I despise your festivals,*
> *and I take no delight in your solemn assemblies...*
> *Take away from me the noise of your songs;*
> *I will not listen to the melody of your harps* (Amos 5:21, 23).

Since the woman is alone, she goes out to find someone who will share the feast, and pretends to the gullible young man that she has come out specially to find him (v. 15). Poignantly, 'seek you eagerly' is the same word as in 1:28, which describes seeking Wisdom 'diligently'. How flattering.

Her home is luxurious. Her bed is covered with Egyptian coverlets (trade between Israel and Egypt was of long standing), and, after the manner of the time, it will have a headboard and a footboard with a plentiful supply of cushions. And to add the final delightful touch, it is sprinkled with the perfume of delicious, imported spices (vv. 16–17).

The invitation, it transpires, is not to share a meal but to indulge in uninhibited sexual pleasure. 'Let us delight ourselves' (literally, "be saturated") with love,' she says; 'let us take our fill of love until morning'—the prospect is of sheer enjoyment.

Shameful inducements

Her husband, apparently a rich merchant called on to make long journeys, will be away for some time—as was the custom, often with disastrous results; see Matthew 24:45–51 for Jesus' story of the master who returned after an absence to find that some of his most trusted servants had been up to no good. The festival of the full moon (Psalm 81:3), when he is expected home (v. 20), is in mid-month; the darkness in which this clandestine meeting takes place suggests that it happens early in the month. So there is little risk of being found out.

Faced with all this, what will a naïve, none-too-intelligent youth do? The rewards of Wisdom are likely to come a poor second to this prospect of ostentation, flattery, good living, and uninhibited physical pleasure.

PRAYER

Lord, I pray for your restraining power on all of us, your children, when we are faced with attractive and overwhelming temptation. Help us to remember that 'the world and its desire are passing away, but those who do the will of God live for ever' (1 John 2:17).

The END *of the* AFFAIR

Predictably, the young man gives in and follows the woman home. The father's wise advice is no match for her 'smooth talk' and 'seductive speech'. 'Persuading' and 'compelling' (v. 21) are words used elsewhere for Israel being led astray to worship idols (1 Kings 11:2, Deuteronomy 13:5); as the youth walks into the trap like a captive animal, there is a dreadful feeling of having seen it all before.

Two powerful pictures in verses 23 and 27 bring home the disastrous consequences of his decision. The adulteress is a murderess as surely as if she stabbed her victim to the heart; and her house is itself an ante-room to Sheol; anyone who steps into it is as good as dead. There is a dreadful finality about this warning. For an inexperienced youth in a big city, the attractions of sexual experiment may be great, but the satisfaction they bring is short-lived. It will end in the irreversible destruction of spirit, mind and body.

The father concludes

Verses 24–27 take up where verse 9 left off. The final appeal is to 'my children', and it repeats the now-familiar warnings about sexual folly—the need to resist the temptation to behave promiscuously, and the dire consequences of yielding to that temptation.

This is the last of the 'fatherly talks' in these opening chapters of Proverbs. Looking back, what impression of family life and parental guidance do they give? The experience of a loving and stable home over two generations (1:8; 4:1–4) is expressed with a wealth of maturity. The words have authority and set clear and confident boundaries; the father has no doubt about his right to advise, or about the rightness of what he says. They are intensely practical and plainspoken (3:1–12). The joys and rewards of finding Wisdom and of fulfilling our duties towards God are clearly set out (2:1–9; 3:1–12), and so are the terrible consequences of yielding to peer pressure and of making the wrong choices (4:10–19). The dangers of promiscuity and adultery are repeatedly emphasized and spelt out in horrifying detail (2:16–19; 5:1–14; 6:20–35; 7:1–9, 24–27).

Above all, this advice tries to encourage a sense of proportion. When we are young it is not easy to see beyond the immediate present, but the fact is that our decisions and what follows from them reach far into the future. The father tries to put them in the context of the whole of life.

We are not told how far all this appeals to the young or influences their behaviour, but one thing is certain: nobody in this family will go to the bad for want of good advice!

TO THINK ABOUT

How can young people keep their way pure?
By guarding it according to your word.
(Psalm 119:9)

PRAYER

Lord, help us all, old or young, to listen to and value the advice of
those who have experience of you and of your ways. Thank you for
the privilege of sharing their friendship and their wisdom.

WISDOM'S PORTRAIT (III)

In chapter 8 we have the full-colour, finished portrait of Wisdom, putting flesh on the pencil sketches of the two previous pictures in 1:20–33 and 3:13–18. It calls for detailed examination. This first section deals with Wisdom's availability and universal appeal.

Maximum publicity is her policy. She 'raises her voice' and demands full attention (v. 1)—not just a hearing for a few moments. She speaks out in the places where people are likely to meet and talk: on the 'heights', or the battlements of the city, where she can be seen; at the crossroads where there is most traffic; and in the city gates, the meeting place for the elders of the town (vv. 2–3). There is nothing furtive about her message. Wherever people are, Wisdom goes. She does not wait for them to come to her.

What she offers is for everybody (vv. 4–5). There is nothing exclusive about Wisdom; she reaches out to all ages, classes and races (v. 4); she is interested in everybody, not only the already skilled and clever who may not seem to need her, but also the 'intellectually challenged', the not-very-bright, the slow learners. She welcomes them all, and all are capable of learning from her (v. 5). For what she has to give is not obscure learning, but basic common sense; to acquire intelligence does not mean to become brighter, but to grasp the basic concepts of right living—a task not beyond any of us.

Wisdom is reliable

Verses 6–9 say the same things several times over—perhaps on the principle that nobody takes anything in after only one telling.

What she says is 'noble', or honest (v. 6), and true—the same root as 'Amen'—something which will stand as solid and trustworthy. She rejects wickedness with horror (v. 7).

Her words are totally honest and straightforward; there is nothing devious or crooked about them (v. 8). 'What you see is what you get.'

And you do not have to be a great brain to understand what she is saying; anybody who has a sense of what is right and wrong will recognize her teaching as consistent (v. 9). So we are not predestined to be either wise or fools; it is a matter of choice. However, since all truths are not self-evident, we do have to be prepared in mind and heart to receive them.

And we are reminded that Wisdom is infinitely precious (vv. 10–11). This is not the first time that her value has been extolled (see 3:13–15), but here it is not the rewards that she brings but she herself, for her own sake, who is commended (v. 11). There is a world of difference between love which is part of enlightened self-interest, however justified, and love which does not think of self-gain.

PRAYER

Lord, when I am not very confident, help me to remember that your gift of Wisdom is not only for the self-assured. And if I am sometimes over-confident in my own ability, help me to continue my search humbly for her, knowing that she always has more to offer. May I never undervalue this precious gift which comes from you. Amen.

The GIFTS *of* WISDOM

It may seem strange in our culture to have someone, however eminent and desirable, extol herself; in the ancient Near East it was not at all unusual for a deity to speak in praise of the gifts he, or sometimes she, will give to her followers. The Canaanite god Baal says, 'I alone am he who will reign over the gods, yea, be leader of the gods and men.'

The ability to cope

Wisdom's associates are eminently desirable. She lives with prudence, and she is intimate with knowledge, discretion, insight, power, and good advice (vv. 12, 14)—the things which in the first seven verses of Proverbs are set out as the basics of a moral and spiritual education, as essential to the wise as the Law is to the priest and the Word is to the prophet. They are all capacities which we need if we are to make sense of life and meet its demands, so we come back to the basic definition of Wisdom as 'the ability to cope'. They are human qualities which it is not beyond anyone to attain, but in the middle of describing them Wisdom points us to God (v. 13). Our moral and intellectual life should be inseparable from the spiritual, from our 'fear of the Lord'—our relationship of loving, reverent obedience with him (1:7)—and from a hatred of everything that is arrogant, evil and crooked.

This echoes the description of the ideal king in Isaiah 11:2:

The spirit of the Lord shall rest on him,
  the spirit of wisdom and understanding,
  the spirit of counsel and might,
  the spirit of knowledge and the fear of the Lord.

Wisdom as a royal counsellor

Kings, rulers and nobles are mentioned elsewhere in Proverbs, and much of its advice is probably directed towards young men who are being trained for high office. On the whole, they are regarded favourably as people to be worked with, needing to be controlled by knowledge and discretion. Is human wisdom enough, or do they need divine Wisdom (vv. 15–16)?

The ideas in Proverbs should perhaps be taken together with those in the Psalms, where the king is often a person to be dealt with cautiously; it is God who is his guide and the source of his effectiveness as a ruler:

> Give the king your justice, O God,
>> and your righteousness to a king's son (Psalm 72:1).

Rewards

The rewards of following Wisdom at first look familiar: riches, good reputation, wealth and well-being (vv. 17–21; see 3:13–15). But they are not purely worldly benefits. Justice and righteousness, that is, being right with God, will help to make and keep things right between people and between nations.

In verse 17 there is something else. Wisdom not only rewards those who follow her; she loves those who love her enough to persevere in their search for her. This is not a conditional promise; it is saying that we must earnestly desire Wisdom if we want to come into an intimate relationship with her, and that if we make this sincere effort, we can be sure of finding her.

TO THINK ABOUT

How highly do I value Wisdom? What sacrifices will I make to be sure of finding her? What difference does she make to my life?

PRAYER

Almighty God, the giver of wisdom, without whose help resolutions are vain, without whose blessing study is ineffectual; enable me, if it be thy will, to attain such knowledge as may qualify me to direct the doubtful and instruct the ignorant; to prevent wrongs and terminate contentions; and grant that I shall use that knowledge which I shall attain, to thy glory and my own salvation.

Samuel Johnson (1709–86)

23 PROVERBS 8:22-31

WISDOM'S LIFE *with* GOD

This paragraph is different in style and language from the rest of the chapter, and is one of the most important in Proverbs. Wisdom, pictured in 3:19–20 as God's agent in creation, becomes his companion from before the beginning of the world, and his skilful, joyful and beloved co-worker in the making of the universe.

Possessed or created?

Was Wisdom created by God, or was she always a part of him? Verses 22–24 can be read either way. 'Created' (v. 22) can also mean 'possessed'; 'set up' (v. 23) and 'brought forth' (v. 24) can be read as 'fashioned' and 'poured out'. What is clear is that Wisdom predates the world; that before it began, she was a partner in God's purposes.

To be able to say 'I was there' at any great event usually secures attention. Wisdom says, 'I was there before and during the creation of the world' (vv. 24–29). Each created element is named in turn—the springs, the mountains, the fields, even the 'world's first bits of soil' (v. 26). In verses 27–29 the actual acts of creation—the dome of the heavens, the 'fountains of the deep', the sky, the boundaries for the sea, the foundations of the earth, echo the poem in Genesis 1.

However, Wisdom was not simply a spectator, she was an active partner (vv. 30–31). This puts the finishing touches to Wisdom's portrait. She was God's 'master worker' (v. 30), his delight (an alternative reading for 'master worker' is 'his child'); rejoicing, or, more accurately, laughing for joy (v. 31).

Upright, intelligent, disciplined, Wisdom has also known creativity, exuberance and inspiration. She takes immense pleasure not only in the world of nature, but in the human race. 'Delighting' (vv. 30, 31) is an intense word.

So who is Wisdom?

We come back to our first question. Is she an attribute of God, is she a created being, or is she the forerunner of the incarnate Son of God?

The New Testament writers have no hesitation in using the idea of Wisdom the creator to fill out what they want to say about Jesus, the wisdom of God (1 Corinthians 1:24), showing him to be the means by which God created the world.

> *Long ago God spoke to our ancestors in many and various ways by the prophets, but in these last days he has spoken to us by a Son... through whom he also created the worlds* (Hebrews 1:1–2).

> *(Jesus) is the image of the invisible God, the firstborn of all creation; for in him all things in heaven and on earth were created... all things have been created through him and for him. He himself is before all things, and in him all things hold together* (Colossians 1:15–17).

Perhaps the most striking identification comes by way of the Old Testament and the literature between the Testaments, which identifies Wisdom first with the Israelite Law and then with the Greek concept of the Word: this leads us to 'In the beginning was the Word, and the Word was with God, and the Word was God. He was in the beginning with God. All things came into being through him, and without him not one thing came into being' (John 1:1–3).

PRAYER

Lord, I may not understand Wisdom fully, but help me to rejoice with her in her work of creation. And lead me, through her, to know more about your Son.

WISDOM'S FINAL APPEAL

Wisdom has made her case in this chapter. She is open, truthful and straight, intelligible, shrewd and strong (vv. 1–9, 12–14).

She has influence on those with great responsibilities (vv. 15–16), but her affection is for anyone—from the highest in the land to the most ordinary—who will receive it (v. 17). Her greatest benefits are beyond earthly wealth (vv. 10–11, 19), yet her followers need be no strangers to prosperity and well-being (vv. 18, 21).

Her life began before the world was made; she was God's co-worker in creation, and the relationship between them was one of joy and delight, a delight which is extended to humanity. In her, the created order and human life blend together in harmony (vv. 22–31). For Christians, her teaching, her activities and her personality foreshadow Jesus.

Now, for the first and only time, she calls her hearers 'my children' (v. 32). What is there left to say?

The way of happiness

This is well known to anyone who has followed her teaching. To listen and take notice, to follow Wisdom's ways, are familiar commands. And this must be habitual.

'Watching daily at my gates, waiting beside my doors' (v. 34) conjures up a picture of being in constant attendance at Wisdom's home. Perhaps the picture is of waiting at the door of someone important, or perhaps the reference is to the house of the wise teacher who gives daily instruction. Either way, there is an implied contrast between this and the house of the adulteress (5:8; 7:27)—one leading to life, the other to death. There is also a sense in which we wait for what Wisdom has to give us—we are not doing her a favour by continually nagging at her.

A matter of choice

Wisdom never forces us; she describes certain situations, puts the options to us, and leaves us to make up our own minds. It is up to us to choose the way of happiness. Our lives are ruled by our own decisions rather than by a moral code. To 'miss' Wisdom (v. 36) means literally to 'miss the mark'—one of the Bible's ways of describing sin; to 'hate' her must be our decision. If we choose this way, it can only be self-destructive. So God's attitude to us is the result of our response to the advice of his counsellor; it is our choice (v. 35).

The question again arises whether we are choosing between physical or spiritual life and death? It looks like the former (see also 1:33; 2:21–22; 3:16), but the two aspects are tied up together. It is a matter of choosing moral as well as physical well-being, or bodily and moral failure and destruction.

PRAYER

Lord, help me in the choices I have to make. Give me the courage and perception always to choose what is positive and life-enhancing, and to reject what will lead to darkness and despair.

25 PROVERBS 9:1–6

An INVITATION *to* ACCEPT

The idea of a feast for the righteous recurs in Scripture, often describing the coming of the Messiah at the end of time. Jesus tells a parable strikingly similar to these verses in Matthew 22:2–10, with its lavish banquet, its spacious house, and its generous, open invitation delivered by hand.

Wisdom's house

The 'seven pillars of Wisdom' (v. 1) have been interpreted in many ways by Jewish and Christian writers. Do they mean the seven 'firmaments' in the heavens, the seven regions or climates, the seven days of creation, the seven books of the Law; or do they foretell the seven sacraments, or even the seven liberal arts? Are they referring to Wisdom's part in creation, and to the contemporary idea of the earth's structure, as in 'When the earth totters, with all its inhabitants, it is I who keep its pillars steady' (Psalm 75:3)?

There is probably no need for any such elaborate explanations. 'Hewn' (v. 1) is better translated 'put in place'; the seven pillars, although reminiscent of the pillars holding up the earth, are more likely to be those surrounding the inner court of a fairly well-to-do house—three on either side, one at the far end. Wisdom is transformed from the joyful collaborator with the divine creator to a busy housewife with a permanent establishment, preparing to give a feast (v. 2).

Wisdom's hospitality

It is usual to send out invitations by messenger (v. 3), but she makes doubly sure that everybody is informed when she calls out from the thoroughfares of the city—the 'highest places' where she can be seen and heard (see 8:2).

Meat and wine (v. 2) are the staples of a banquet. Meat, only eaten as a rule at religious festivals, is a special treat; wine is mixed with spices to make it more pleasant to the taste. However, the loaded table and the festive menu represent not physical food and drink, but moral and mental nourishment. The 'simple'—those with unformed, wide-open minds, not particularly sinful but susceptible to sin's

64

influence—and those 'without sense' are specially invited (v. 4). This does not mean that the firmly established righteous and the seriously evil are excluded, but they are not specifically mentioned, perhaps because the good do not need guidance and the wicked will not accept it. Wisdom is nothing if not realistic.

The offer is the gift of a long, prosperous and happy life, blessed with the faculty of insight, or discernment (v. 6). But to come to the feast and receive Wisdom's generosity, the easily led, undiscriminating guests must relinquish their state of blissful ignorance and grow up. Wisdom is not for the immature.

TO THINK ABOUT

'Lay aside immaturity and live' is an instruction which the New Testament not only echoes but enlarges upon. 'We must no longer be children, tossed to and fro and blown about by every wind of doctrine, by people's trickery, by their craftiness in deceitful scheming. But speaking the truth in love, we must grow up in every way into him who is the head, into Christ'.
(Ephesians 4:14–15)

PRAYER

Lord, thank you for your gracious invitation to be your guest. I am grateful and honoured to be given the chance to enjoy all your promised blessings.

An INVITATION *to* REFUSE

This passage makes a striking contrast with verses 1–6, which we have just read. We shall come back to verses 7–12 later.

The rival to Wisdom's invitation to her feast is issued by Folly, 'the Lady Stupidity', as the Revised English Bible calls her. Her part is in some ways similar to that played by Wisdom in verses 1–6. She appears conspicuously in public and invites all who pass by, whether casual wayfarers or people set on an errand, to join her (vv. 14–16). Wisdom sends out invitations, Folly sits at the door of her house; both are equally earnest and equally pressing.

However, the likeness ends here. 'The foolish woman' literally means 'the woman of folly', a word associated with the 'scoffers' of 1:22—not the inexperienced and gullible, not those openly contemptuous of moral and religious truth, but those who are insensible to it. So although Folly is loud, or 'boisterous' (v. 13), she is ignorant. She is not necessarily unintelligent, but she knows nothing worth knowing about right and wrong. Other versions have 'she knows not what' or 'she knows not shame'—the picture is of a loud-mouthed, insensitive moral ignoramus. Unlike Wisdom, who takes trouble to seek out guests, she invites anyone who happens to be passing, promising them secret, clandestine pleasures. Verse 17 is probably a popular proverb: the things forbidden by law or condemned by society are all the more tempting because they are prohibited.

Who is Folly?

Is she the same as the adulteress of chapters 5 and 7, and are the delights she offers those of illicit sex? Or is she symbolic of something deeper and more fundamental? Commentators differ on this point. Her seat at the door of her house is the traditional position of the prostitute, and her blandishments put us in mind of the woman whose 'husband is not at home' and who entices the inexperienced youth with, 'Come, let us take our fill of love until morning; let us delight ourselves with love' (7:18). The enjoyment of sexual immorality is surely best experienced in secret.

Or, since adultery is a symbol of wilful folly in general, do these warnings encompass something much more general—a whole attitude towards life and behaviour contrasting with Wisdom's invitation to maturity and understanding?

Whichever interpretation we prefer, the result is the same. Folly's house is actually part of the underworld, and her guests, once they enter, are as good as dead. So the simple young, responding to her inducements and not knowing their danger, are irrevocably doomed (v. 18).

Inescapable decisions

These two invitations bring into sharp relief the choices which we face repeatedly when we read these first nine chapters of Proverbs. Do we choose rectitude or debauchery, insight or ignorance, moral understanding or moral insensitivity, long-term self-discipline or immediate gratification? The options are clearly stated; the decision must be ours.

TO THINK ABOUT

We confront the same choice as that which Moses offered the Children of Israel: 'See, I have set before you today life and prosperity, death and adversity... Choose life.'
(Deuteronomy 30:15, 19)

PRAYER

Lord, so often I am attracted by what I know in my heart is wrong. Give me the insight and the maturity to choose your way.

SOME PERSONAL ADVICE

This section comes between the invitations of Wisdom and Folly: it may have been meant to spell out the implications of accepting Wisdom's call, much as verse 18 spells out the consequences of saying 'Yes' to Folly. It contrasts the different ways in which 'the scoffer' and 'the wise' receive advice.

The 'scoffer'

Youth is often the time when, in seeking to establish our own values, and influenced by the prevailing culture and intense peer pressure, we question the values taught us by our parents and the 'given' structure of morality. But this need not mean that we reject everything from the past—such an attitude leads to pride and cynicism, and to destructive and hurtful behaviour. If we take that path, we join the 'scoffers'. We have met the scoffer before (1:22) and we shall meet him (or her) later—full of the pride that leads to trouble (21:24), and making mischief in the community (22:10). He is one who openly despises and mocks what is good, not through lack of intelligence like the simple, or through moral insensitivity like the fool, but from deliberate choice. He is one of the saddest figures in Proverbs, because he has made himself virtually ineducable. Nobody likes to be rebuked, but the scoffer meets any attempt at correction with abuse (7–8a), hatred and even violence ('hurt' in verse 7 means 'physically blemished'). He seems incapable of profiting from teaching, and it is best not to reason with him.

Wisdom through reverence for God

The wise (vv. 8b–11) have the grace to receive a rebuke with gratitude, and so they learn from it and 'become wiser still' (v. 9). Because of their humility, they are equated with the righteous, or upright. But the real secret of their progress is the fear of the Lord. 'Beginning' (v. 10) is not the same word as in 1:7; here, it means 'the first principle' rather than the 'first step' in the learning process. But both verses make the point that all wisdom starts from reverence for God. This is the one verse in chapter 9 which refers directly to God. It is a reminder that we can only attain Wisdom if we serve him, and that if we yield to Folly we reject him.

For a moment Wisdom speaks again (v. 11) with the now-familiar promise of long life for her followers, 'by me'. Some ancient versions have 'For by it your days will be multiplied', assuming that verses 10 and 11 are not spoken directly by Wisdom, but the sense is the same whichever reading we take.

Where it all ends

Our lives are influenced by others, but in the end, we are responsible for our own decisions.

Ezekiel 18:4 sets out the doctrine of individual responsibility: 'Know that all lives are mine; the life of the parent as well as the life of the child is mine: it is only the person who sins that shall die.'

This truth is sharply reinforced here (v. 12). Those who choose Wisdom will reap her rewards; those who reject her must bear the consequences, and it will be a lonely business.

PRAYER

*Lord, I do not find it easy to accept correction; please give me
the humility to learn from it. Keep me from the arrogance
which leads to 'hardness of heart and contempt of thy word
and commandment'.*

28   PROVERBS 10:1—22:16

WISE SAYINGS

Now there is a change of style. We no longer have the father addressing the child, or the discourses by or about Wisdom. Instead, we
have a series of what often look like disconnected one-liners—traditional proverbs, or wise, pithy remarks, headed 'the proverbs of
Solomon'. Various attempts have been made to impose some sort of
structure on these sayings. Is there a distinction between those for
the benefit of the individual, those for the benefit of the community,
and those about behaviour explicitly related to God? Is there a development in thinking, from chapters 10—15 where references to God
are rare, to 16:1—22:16 where they are more frequent? Is it significant that in chapters 10—15, 163 out of 183 sayings contrast one
thing with another, whereas in the later chapters there is more comparison than contrast? Or are some of the connections purely by
word association?

Sometimes we seem to spot a theme: in chapter 10 there are a
number of sayings about speech and silence, and 16:10–15 is mostly
about kings. But on the whole, it is probably best to take the
thoughts as they come—as a reflection of life, which after all is not
tidy or easy to categorize. This method of considering ethical and
spiritual matters does not begin with doctrine and then apply it to
everyday things; it starts with the practical business of living, and
goes on to develop thinking about principles and behaviour and
beliefs. Nothing is too ordinary to be included: the family, education,
animal life, finance, quarrelling and harmony, food and drink, drunkenness and sobriety are all here. Many ideas are not what we might
see as spiritual; some of them make us laugh, most of them strike a
chord in our own experience. But they all provoke thought, and, after
the thought, we may find that a prayer comes into our minds.

Parents and children, wealth and poverty, hard work and laziness
(10:1–5) are three comparisons which will recur in these 'proverbs of
Solomon'—some of which probably come from Solomon's time,
though none of them can be proved to have come from Solomon
himself.

Parents and children

It is stating the obvious to say that wisdom in a child, with its associations of righteousness and happiness, brings joy to the family (v. 1), while foolishness, whether in the form of immaturity, insensitivity or outright rebellion, brings grief. The way the proverb is framed might be read as meaning that the father is more interested in the wise child and the mother in the foolish, but 'father' and 'mother' both stand for 'parents'.

Wealth and poverty

Ill-gotten wealth may bring temporary success, but profits nothing in the end (v. 2) since, unlike an upright life, it cannot give any protection against the divine or human retribution which will overtake the offender. On the other hand, righteousness, or integrity, has the blessing of God. So, while wealth will not avert God's judgment, righteousness secures his favour.

In verse 3, the Old Testament conviction that the nation of Israel, or at least the godly part of it, will be protected by divine justice through all its changing fortunes (a point of view expounded in detail in Isaiah 7 and Ezekiel 36) is applied to the individual. The material needs of the righteous will be provided by God.

Hard work and laziness

Since 'hand' often refers to an actual person, verse 4 could read 'The lazy become poor, the diligent become rich'—the Protestant work ethic baldly stated. Proverbs has no time for the 'idle rich'; even kings have their job to do. However, verse 5 can be developed in a less simplistic way. The contrast between the behaviour of the hard-working and the lazy child at a busy period in a farming family ('harvest' and 'summer' are both used for the time of reaping) can be extended first to any child who has the sort of qualities of which parents approve, and then to the way in which times of pressure reveal our true character.

TO THINK ABOUT

How often do we stop and think about the ordinary events of our lives? If we look, can we see in them some lessons to learn, or some dangers to avoid?

BLESSINGS

The benefits of a life of integrity are described in verses 6, 7 and 9. The 'blessings' of verse 6 may be those of a good reputation, or those bestowed by God; traditionally, hands were placed on the head of one receiving a blessing (see Genesis 48:14–22, where Jacob blesses his grandsons). 'The mouth of the wicked conceals violence' comes again in verse 11, where it makes more sense. Here 'conceals' could read 'is filled with'—that is, in contrast with the joys of the righteous, the wicked will suffer harm, like someone who by reckless foolishness 'drinks violence'.

Reputation after as well as before death is important in a society without a very developed doctrine of the hereafter. 'Name' and 'memory' (v. 7) mean the same, so just as the godly are remembered with honour, the ungodly's reputation will become rotten and decayed, like their flesh and bones.

But as well as blessing now and honour hereafter, an upright life brings security (v. 9). The honest have nothing to fear, the crooked and devious will be exposed. In other words, 'Be sure your sin will find you out.'

Wise and foolish talk

The right and wrong use of speech, another frequent topic in 10:1—22:16, is the other subject of verses 8 and 10–14. The 'wise of heart', or the right-minded, submit themselves to authority (v. 8), whether human or divine. They are not afraid to speak out against what is wrong (v. 10), and their reproof, openly given, enriches relationships in family and community because it is inspired by love (v. 12). So love can 'cover' the offences of others, not by condoning them but by making allowances. 'Love covers a multitude of offences', quoted in 1 Peter 4:8, is about forgiveness as well as kindness. The same idea of putting sin out of sight is applied elsewhere in the Old Testament to God:

Happy are those whose transgression is forgiven,
  whose sin is covered (Psalm 32:1).

The words of the wise, like their lives, are guided by reason (v. 13). They treasure up, or conceal, knowledge until it is appropriate to speak; they do not talk for the sake of it (v. 14). So what they say is a blessing to others, just as a drink of fresh water from a fountain (always preferred to a cistern which only stores water) will strengthen a weary traveller (v. 11).

The foolish, thoughtless talkers are a contrast in every way. They are often motivated by hatred and are concerned to make trouble (v. 12). They communicate by body language as well as by words: malicious looks and hints stir up trouble in a community—not only dissension but pain. The word for 'strife' means literally 'grief'. Their 'mouth', or speech, conceals their real thoughts; alternatively, violence—oppressive, high-handed conduct—clothes them like a garment, controlling what they say and how they act. Their lives as well as their tongues are out of control; lacking a sense of direction, they invariably get into trouble (v. 13). Worst of all, by their relentless, ignorant chattering they bring ruin on themselves (v. 8) and disaster on others (v. 14). The word for ruin is only used here and in Hosea 4:14, which says, 'A people without understanding comes to ruin.'

PRAYER

Lord, so often I cannot seem to control my tongue, and I say thoughtless and hurtful things. Please help me to remember the example of Jesus, who 'did not return abuse, but entrusted himself to the one who judges justly' (1 Peter 2:23).

WEALTH & POVERTY

Two of the earlier themes of this chapter are picked up. First, there are more sayings about wealth and poverty.

Verse 15 is a statement of fact, without any moral implications. The dangers of wealth, and the duties of society to the poor, are dealt with elsewhere (11:4; 19:17). Wealth protects us from certain kinds of misfortune, while poverty makes us vulnerable to physical and social ills. The moral teaching comes in verse 16. What we earn (and there is no reason to suppose that the 'gain' of the wicked is ill-gotten in this case), used rightly, can bring long life and earthly happiness. But misused it leads to sin with its threat of punishment and ultimately of death.

Best of all is the prosperity that comes with God's blessing (v. 22)—one of the rare references to God in this chapter. All the good things that are attributed to the honesty of the righteous or the prudence of the wise come ultimately from him. The second half of the verse can be interpreted in two ways—either, 'Wealth bestowed by God is different from ill-gotten gain because it is free from sorrow, rather than bringing evil with it', or (reading 'toil' for 'sorrow'), 'All the work in the world cannot add to what God has already given'.

Whichever reading we choose, the meaning seems to be not that labour in itself is useless, but that labour without divine blessing is worse than useless:

Unless the Lord builds the house,
　those who build it labour in vain.
Unless the Lord guards the city,
　the guard keeps watch in vain (Psalm 127:1).

Listening and speaking

Listening to other people is as important as speaking ourselves. The 'instruction' and 'rebuke' of verse 17 is the teaching of the parent or mentor so carefully set out in chapters 1—9. The one who is disciplined by correction is the one who is likely to be spiritually and materially successful; the one who rejects reproof, whether simple, a fool or a scoffer (see 1:22), will find that resistance is a hindrance to progress of any kind.

Malice and unkind gossip are condemned. Anyone who hates in secret is a liar; anyone who expresses hatred in slanderous terms is a fool (v. 18). But it is equally important to use the power of speech constructively—and preferably sparingly. 'Transgression', or offence against others, often comes from saying too much rather than saying too little (v. 19). The rabbis' advice was, 'Silence is a hedge about wisdom.'

More positively, the thought and speech of the righteous (equated with the wise) are both valuable in themselves and of benefit to others, while the foolish and the wicked not only speak what is of 'little worth' (a contemptuous expression), but can barely sustain themselves, much less nurture anyone else (vv. 20–21).

TO THINK ABOUT

Value men, not by their wealth and preferment in the world, but by their virtue. Good men are good for something. As long as they have a mouth to speak, that will make them valuable and useful… they will enrich those that hear them with wisdom. (But) he that is of the earth speaks of the earth, and neither understands nor relishes the things of God.

Matthew Henry (1662–1714)

FINDING *the* LORD'S WAY

Verse 26, like verse 15, states the obvious in an entertaining way. Our friend the lazybones reappears. Not only is he at fault, his irritating effect upon his employer is like that of sour wine which sets his teeth on edge or smoke which makes his eyes smart.

There are a number of contrasts in this passage. The first is between right and wrong conduct (v. 23). Fools, superficial in their moral and intellectual judgments, have no sense of sin but see wrongdoing as part of human nature—a normal, enjoyable activity. These are not trivial offences, but wickedness—a strong word implying the enormity of the behaviour and attitudes it describes. Yet they are actually a delight to their perpetrators—the same word as is used in 8:30-31 to describe God's relationship to Wisdom and her part in the creation of the world. On the other hand, anyone of discernment will find a natural pleasure in behaving wisely and doing what is right.

The contrast between the destiny of the righteous and the wicked follows (vv. 24-25, 27-31). In the matter of happiness, which everyone desires, the righteous will have their wish (v. 24). We might expect the second half of the verse simply to say that the wicked will not have their wish, but the contrast is expressed more vividly: they will be overtaken by the calamity which they fear. This thought is repeated in verse 28: the righteous will, and the wicked will not, see the fulfilment of their hopes.

The righteous have stability—their foundations of belief and behaviour go so deep that nothing will shake them—but the wicked are like an unstable building (v. 25). Jesus makes the same point in the story of the houses built on rock and on sand (Matthew 7: 24-27).

So while the reverent obedience to God of a righteous person leads to a long life (whether by God's decree or by the moderate nature of their lifestyle is not stated), the wicked have no such expectations (v. 27).

Not only stability but security is promised to the righteous (v. 29–30). 'The way of the Lord' is not usually described as a 'stronghold'; the Revised Standard Version has 'The Lord is a stronghold', which is easier to understand. God's government of the world produces predictable results: protection is given to the righteous but withheld from the wicked, and the privilege of citizenship will be given to the former but not to the latter. The relationship between God, the people and the land of Canaan is a constant theme in the Old Testament. It is always understood that the final blessing to Israel will come in the promised land, so 'remaining in the land' means being granted the highest privilege—something denied to the ungodly.

Speech and consequences

What people say also has consequences (vv. 31–32). The 'mouth', or 'speech' of the righteous 'brings forth wisdom'—that is, it sprouts or grows, like a tree bearing fruit. 'Cut off'—the fate promised to the tongue of the wicked—can mean 'cut down', the idea of the unfruitful tree which also appears in the fourth Gospel (John 15:2).

Verse 32 is not about consequences, but states the difference between two types of speech—the acceptable, which gives pleasure to others or to God, and the devious and crooked, which is likely to stir up strife. This does not imply that the righteous try only to please, but that they use sincere and kindly words which often pour oil on troubled waters.

This chapter raises the problem which arose previously (see 3:11–12) and which will recur. Happiness, long life and prosperity are not the inevitable consequences of goodness; quite the reverse—it is often the devious and unprincipled who flourish. And since Proverbs is concerned with this life rather than the next, we cannot say that it is talking about reward and punishment after death. Do the authors make their point so often and so vehemently hoping that they will restrain evil and encourage good? But dire warnings have seldom acted as a deterrent. There is no answer to this dilemma, except to remember that other Old Testament writers are aware of it (read Psalms 37 and 73), and to trust in the ultimate justice and mercy of God.

PRAYER

Lord, often I do not understand your ways, but help me to trust you all the same.

32   PROVERBS 11:1–11

HUMILITY & HONESTY

The question of integrity in business is raised in verse 1. Giving short measure, either by tampering with the scales or by an inaccurate weight (the word is 'stone', since stones were used as weights) was common in the ancient Near East, and was universally unacceptable. Amen-em-opet declares that this kind of crime is 'an abomination to (the god) Re'. In the Bible, the Law condemns it (Leviticus 19: 35–36), and the prophets speak out against it (Micah 6:11).

The choice is offered: indulge in a dishonest practice which is an 'abomination' to God (originally used in a ritual sense, when there was something wrong with a sacrifice), or deal honestly and give him pleasure. Here, for once, no material reward is promised, only that which comes from any upright life—wisdom (vv. 2, 9), a clear purpose and a clear conscience (vv. 3, 5), fulfilment and safety (v. 6), and the chance to be of benefit to the community (vv. 10–11).

Pride goes before a fall

An overweening sense of our own importance, and the arrogant behaviour which goes with it, makes enemies, and leads to downfall (v. 2). True humility (the word only appears here, relating to other people, and in Micah 6:8 relating to God) is co-operative and avoids antagonism. So it is a form of wisdom applied to human relationships.

Righteousness and wickedness

Verses 3–6 all make the same point, but make it in slightly different ways. The teaching is what we have already met and will meet again—that righteousness leads to a long and happy life, while wickedness leads to death and destruction.

'Integrity' (v. 3) is the same word as in 10:9, meaning 'wholeness' or 'soundness'. 'Crookedness', or 'turning upside down' is only found here and in 15:4; it is more radical than 'deviation', it is a total reversal of right values.

The 'day of wrath' (v. 4) can mean any impending catastrophe. For the prophets, the idea has national significance, as the day on which God will punish the sin of Israel by famine, defeat or exile. In

Wisdom literature it usually means the 'moment of truth' for the individual. The picture of the righteous treading a straight, or smooth, path (v. 5) is that of 3:6; when the wicked stray, they stumble and fall. Goodness is socially helpful (v. 6), but the wicked are their own worst enemies. They bring about their own downfall by their 'schemes' (literally, their evil desires—the 'craving'of 10:3).

Careful reading required

Each of verses 7–9 can easily be misunderstood. Verse 7 is unusual in this chapter because it does not make a contrast; its two parts reinforce each other. Death puts an end to all the hopes and expectations of the wicked and the godless. There is something tragic as well as immoral about the 'godless'; the word comes from a root meaning 'trouble' and 'sorrow'—the name given by Rachel to her younger child, 'Son of my sorrow' (Genesis 35:18).

Verse 8 reads as if the wicked bear the troubles of the righteous, but this would be a complete reversal of the teaching that the righteous suffer for the unrighteous, which reaches its highest expression in the death of Jesus. Rather, it is saying that the troubles that are avoided by right living will inevitably follow wrongdoing.

In verse 9, the righteous escape the ruin which the godless by their destructive speech actually design for them; they are saved by 'knowledge'—a more down-to-earth word than Wisdom, meaning either a general acquaintance with the ways of the world or knowing what the godless are up to and taking avoiding action.

Individual and community

Verses 10 and 11 make plain that what one person does affects everybody else. This corporate view of life is found in the prophets (Amos 4:1–3; Micah 3:9–12), but to them the unit is the nation, and the chief sin is the worship of idols. Here the unit is the city—perhaps influenced by the Greek city-state—and the sin is moral, not specifically religious. But the idea is the same: goodness brings joy to a community, just as wickedness brings weakness and disaster; the triumph of right living and the defeat of wrongdoing are equally applauded.

PRAYER

Lord, help me to remember that none of us lives to ourselves, and that everything I do and say affects someone else.

DANGEROUS TALK

Careless speech is the subject of verses 12 and 13. Lack of regard for someone else (v. 12) may be shown in a number of ways, physical and psychological; here, since it is contrasted with silence, it must involve speech. No distinction is made between deserved and undeserved criticism; contemptuous talk is in itself wrong and foolish. It is wise to keep quiet, not only for reasons of kindness but because of the damage to relationships caused by speaking slightingly of anyone.

Gossip (v. 13) does not sound as serious, but the tale bearers who like to circulate the latest items of scandal are just as dangerous and damaging to reputations as those who spread slander. The gossip cannot be trusted with secrets, whereas the trustworthy will never betray a confidence, whether personal or connected with matters of state.

The message of these verses is that unkind and careless talk is a menace not only to individuals but to a whole community.

The Ship of State

'Guidance' means literally 'steering' (v. 14), and it is assumed here that it is good and skilful. The counsellor had a respected position at court, and expected that his advice would be taken. Ahithopel, a royal counsellor whose counsel was rejected, actually committed suicide (2 Samuel 17:23). However, here the meaning may simply be that in a well-governed city or community questions of policy should be looked at from all sides, and the more opinions available the better. People are resistant to having decisions forced upon them, and securing co-operation often means a great deal of time-consuming consultation.

Rewards and punishments

These are once again dealt with in verses 15–21, with one or two extra ideas. Standing surety (v. 15) has the same consequence as in 6:1–2, except that the guarantee is not for one's neighbour but for the 'stranger'—whether of a different nationality, family or household.

The NRSV follows the Greek text of verse 16, and makes two contrasts. Graciousness brings honour; disregard for virtue brings shame. Timidity, or laziness, leads to poverty; aggressiveness, or vigour, is required if we are to prosper.

The Hebrew reads differently:

A gracious woman gets honour,
  violent (men) obtain wealth.

This is the only place in Proverbs where men and women are contrasted, setting courtesy against brute force. According to this politically incorrect version, the unscrupulous man gains wealth but no reputation; the gracious woman (here, meaning the woman who finds acceptance because of her poise and attitude) gets both—presumably in her own right, since there is no mention of benefit to her husband or family.

The practical good sense of kindness, rather than cruelty as a policy, is emphasized in verse 17, rather than the ennobling effect of one quality and the degrading effect of the other, just as the payment for work done is 'real', or lasting, for the righteous, but is illusory and temporary for the wicked (v. 18).

The now-familiar thoughts about what is pleasing and unacceptable to God, and about life and death, are repeated (vv. 19–21), but with additional emphasis in verse 21. 'Be assured' means literally 'hand to hand'; the traditional way of striking a bargain. 'So,' says the author, 'take my word for it that what I am saying will come about.'

TO THINK ABOUT

This passage is full of certainties, and the constant promise
of rewards in this life for goodness and punishment for wickedness
is not so easy. It may be helpful to think about verse 17,
which points out that the best and worst that can happen to us
is what we do to ourselves. We have to live with the consequences
of our own choices.

34   PROVERBS 11:22–31

An AMUSING CONTRAST

Verse 22 is probably a popular saying. The nose ring was a traditional female ornament, both elegant and valuable. Isaac produces a 'gold nose ring weighing a half shekel' (about a quarter of an ounce) as a gift for Rebekah (Genesis 24:22). A thing of such beauty and worth in a pig's snout is compared to outward loveliness which is not accompanied by 'good sense', (literally 'taste', or discretion, covering both intellectual and moral judgment)—a severe though entertaining variation on 'Beauty is only skin deep'. There is a distressing incongruity when physical beauty is not enhanced by sound judgment.

Nourished by generosity

Liberality and meanness are dealt with in verses 25, 26 and 29. There is generosity in giving, which brings blessing. The generous person 'grows fat', an expression used for well-nourished animal and vegetable life (Jeremiah 31:14; Isaiah 30:23), and giving to others is returned in kind (v. 25)—here in an agricultural society, but equally in any community. On the other hand, to hold back from giving what is only appropriate in the circumstances gives no benefit, but rather leads to poverty (v. 26).

There is generosity in commerce. The black market is not a modern invention: it was quite usual for the wealthy to hoard grain in order to sell it at a high price at a time of scarcity, unmoved by the suffering of others. This practice is wrong: it is the moral duty of the rich to put their goods on the market at the proper price (v. 26).

And there is generosity in the family (v. 29). Those who fail to nourish or build up their households, whether through inability, negligence or niggardliness, will find their reserves reduced to nothing— 'a breath of air'. As a result of this economic and moral folly, they will find themselves working as slaves for the thrifty and successful 'wise'.

Like green leaves

The consequences of our actions are again spelled out (vv. 23, 27–28, 30–31), using illustrations from nature. The righteous flourish 'like green leaves' (v. 28)—an expression similar to that in Psalm 1:3; the effect of their actions is that of a life-giving tree (see 3:18), unlike the

82

enervating and destructive consequences of violence (vv. 28, 30). The chapter ends on a note of absolute certainty—'If… how much more'—which finds an echo, though perhaps less confidently, in 1 Peter 4:18: 'If it is hard for the righteous to be saved, what will become of the ungodly and the sinners?'

The author has no doubt that we reap what we sow, and that we can look for the harvest at some time in our life on earth. We are urged to be generous in all aspects of our lives, but this generosity must be spontaneous if it is to be effective and acceptable.

TO THINK ABOUT

Each of you must give as you have made up your mind, not reluctantly or under compulsion, for God loves a cheerful giver.
(2 Corinthians 9:7)

PRAYER

Lord, help me to be generous in every aspect of my life. Show what I should give to you not only in money but also in time. Teach me how to serve you not only in church but in my work and in the family. I want to use and develop what you have given to me, so that I can be of use to you.

TWO *by* TWO

Every verse in this section presents a contrast.

Two attitudes to education appear in verse 1. 'Discipline' is used in the academic sense of something to which we must apply ourselves (1:2); 'rebuke' or 'admonition' is a necessary part of it. The 'stupid' or 'brutish' not only dislike admonition (who doesn't?) but reject it. The educators may be parents, friends, or 'the wise' who formulate rules for living. But whoever they are, their best efforts will be useless without the active participation of the pupil.

Two relationships with God (v. 2): on the one hand, those of the good, or upright, who gain his favour; and on the other, those who are pronounced guilty ('condemns' is a legal term) because their plans are, by their own choice, evil.

Two prospects (vv. 3, 7) with which we are already familiar are security and uncertainty. The illustration of roots and foundations has already been used in 10:25 and 30. Verse 7 may be about family: the 'house' of the righteous will continue, but the wicked will cease to exist because there will be no descendants to carry on their name—a frightening state of affairs from which there is no hope of restoration.

Two wives are contrasted in verse 4—part of the recurring theme of family in the Wisdom literature. The word translated 'good' is applied to women only four times in the Old Testament—three times in Proverbs and once in Ruth (3:11). It means literally 'vigorous' or 'of good, vigorous character'. Here and in 31:10-31, where the qualities of the ideal wife are set out in detail, it seems to combine virtue with capability—life-enhancing qualities. The wife is responsible for the economic management of the household, and plays her part in the education of the children (1:8, 6:20); her affection is long remembered (3:2). Best of all is her relationship with her husband. She is described as his 'crown', conferring a royal honour on him, so by her character and behaviour she brings him happiness at home and good reputation abroad. However, the wife who does not have this spirit of co-operation and love can destroy her husband's happiness and the whole framework of his life—just as decay destroys the bones, the framework of the body.

Good or bad?

Two sets of thoughts and ideas are the subject of verses 5 and 6. Thoughts, words, advice and speech are all neutral terms; they can be good or bad. Here, as we might expect, the thoughts of the righteous reflect justice; the counsel of the wicked, deceit and treachery. Even more striking is the contrast between the words of the wicked and the upright. The wicked set a trap for the upright by making false accusations which lie in wait like assassins, but the victims are able to escape by making a skilful defence. Notice that here the wicked ambush others, but the righteous save themselves.

Two kinds of behaviour, one acceptable, the other unacceptable, are spelled out in verse 8. Everyone wants approval, but the question is, whose approval? 'Good sense', the 'wise dealing' of 1:3, is not universally popular, but it wins acceptance from those who are honest and upright. Perverted or twisted thinking (the word is used only here in the Old Testament), on the other hand, has no chance of gaining respect from anyone of discernment.

Two sets of circumstances are described in verse 9, the gist of which is that comfort is better than show. To be 'despised' reflects upon someone's social position. David, when offered the king's daughter in marriage, says, 'I am a poor man and of no repute' (1 Samuel 18:23).

However, those of small social importance, provided they can afford a servant (at that time regarded as a basic necessity), are better placed than those who are full of their own importance and position (literally 'who honour themselves') and yet lack the basic necessities of life.

PRAYER

Lord, when I am faced with two alternatives, whether in thought, speech, attitude or action, help me to choose the one which is acceptable to you.

KINDNESS & INDUSTRY

A great deal is said in Proverbs about kind words and actions directed towards people, but the Old Testament also recognizes that consideration must be shown to animals. In the fourth Commandment, which is about keeping the Sabbath as a day of rest, 'livestock' are included (Exodus 20:10)—perhaps inevitably, as they can only work when people work. However, there is a more specific command to be generous in Deuternomy 25:4: 'You shall not muzzle an ox while it is treading out the grain.'

Verse 10 is a reminder that God cares for all living creatures, and not solely for human beings: 'You save humans and animals alike, O Lord' (Psalm 36:6). The second half of the verse is difficult: 'mercy' means 'gentleness' or 'lovingkindness', and how can this be cruel? Possibly it means that even the best efforts at kindness by the wicked are inadequate, and must be regarded as cruelty.

Verse 11 need not be read as special praise for agriculture—it can apply to commerce or politics—but in an agricultural society it illustrates the desirability of pursuing a settled, legitimate occupation. 'Worthless pursuits' does not mean idleness or laziness, but purposeless and pointless occupations, which are not an intelligent choice.

Cause and effect

Verse 12 as it stands is hard to comprehend; it reads, 'The wicked desire the net of the evil.' If we take it literally, it must mean that the wicked seek to enrich themselves through immoral gain, and presumably do not succeed because it is the righteous who are soundly rooted and enjoy the fruits of their labours. But even this has its problems, since a 'root' does not usually bear fruit.

Alternatively, we can read with the RSV:

> *The strong tower of the wicked comes to ruin,*
>   *but the root of the righteous stands firm.*

This makes sense, but involves taking liberties with the Hebrew text.

The 'transgression of their lips' (v. 13) warns us that any malicious talk will bring us into danger by making enemies, whereas the guarded, kindly speech of the righteous can have a healing effect. So we must all take the consequences of our words and deeds (v. 14). 'Manual labour', or 'the work of one's hands', means work in general. We are responsible for what we say and what we do.

Verse 15 and 16 tell us to look out for two marks of a fool. First, there is stupid obstinacy. Fools (see 1:3) are not open to guidance because they do not see the need for it, whereas the wise are prepared to consider advice. Second, there is the habit of reacting angrily and hastily—'on the spot', or 'on the very day'. This is not about forgiveness, 'turning the other cheek' or condoning wrong; it is about self-control.

Use of the tongue

There are more than one hundred verses in Proverbs about the use of the tongue, which emphasizes the power and importance of words.

Evidence in court is the subject of verse 17. It states the obvious, but the fact that it states it at all, together with the prominence given to perjury in Proverbs, suggests that there was a real problem at the time.

'Rash words' or 'chatter' (v. 18) means hasty, ill-advised speech, used of anyone finding themselves unwittingly bound by an oath (Leviticus 5:4), and of Moses when 'he spoke words that were rash' (Psalm 106:33).

This sort of talk need not be malicious, but it can stab like a sword-thrust because it is without thought or regard for anyone's feelings. By contrast, suffering can be eased by a wise, sympathetic word.

'Truth will out' sums up verse 19. Falsehood, on the other hand, unsupported by facts, lasts only a moment—literally 'while I blink'. In view of the persistence of untruths, we can only suppose that the author is taking a long view.

PRAYER

Lord, these are high standards and I cannot reach them without you. Please guide me so that I speak and act in obedience to your will.

87

37 PROVERBS 12:20–28

FINDING PEACE *with* GOD

Truth and lies are contrasted in verses 20 and 22. When people deliberately plan evil (v. 20), the lack of honesty which is part of injustice must be in their nature. On the other hand, 'counsellors of peace' (see 11:14), who plan prosperity and wholeness for others (REB: 'seek the common good'), find pleasure and satisfaction. They can count themselves one with God, who says:

As I have designed,
  so shall it be;
and as I have planned,
  so shall it come to pass (Isaiah 14:24).

Lying (see 6:17), like dishonest dealings (11:1), wickedness (8:7) and crooked ways (11:20), is totally unacceptable to God (v. 22); but faithfulness, or reliability, like honesty (11:1) and indeed Wisdom herself (8:30), is a delight to him.

Reassurance is the key thought in verse 21. 'Harm' contains an element of what is 'sent' or 'allowed'. It is easy to believe this verse when things go well; more difficult in times of trouble. Against Job's friends who firmly believed that suffering, even apparently undeserved suffering, was a punishment for sin, we set Romans 8:28: 'We know that all things work together for good for those who love God.'

Caution and discretion

Discretion and kindness in speech are advised in verses 23 and 25 (see 10:19). If we are shrewd, we will hold knowledge in reserve rather than making fools of ourselves by showing off. Caution is not only common sense, it is in our own interests. However, there is a time when it is right to speak. A good word spoken to someone weighed down by anxiety (v. 25) cannot always remove the cause for concern or fear, but it can lighten the load by sympathy and encouragement.

Verse 24, like 10:4, tells us that hard work brings success, but it extends the thought to a whole workforce or even a nation. The industrious are likely to be in charge of others, the lazy will be forced to work by others. 'Forced labour' was not unknown in Solomon's time—see 1 Kings 9:15–21; on the other hand, this may refer to slavery in general.

Turning to verses 26–28, we find that a part of each is difficult to translate, but the gist is fairly clear. Verse 26 can read, 'The righteous search out' (that is, study) 'their friends', which can either mean giving guidance or taking time to assess new acquaintances. The KJV has '(the righteous) is more excellent than his neighbour', the RSV 'turns away from evil', the REB 'are freed from evil'. There is no 'correct' version, but the message seems to be that the righteous behave sensibly and honourably and the wicked stray from the right way.

Verse 27 can read, 'The lazy do not roast' or 'The lazy do not hunt' their game. The general sense is that the lazy cannot be bothered to provide for themselves while, by contrast, the industrious prosper.

The first part of verse 28 is easy to understand (see 3:2; 8:35), but the second half can read either '(the) journey of its pathway—no death', or '(the) journey of its pathway—to death', presumably meaning the way of unrighteousness. Clearly we are being told to follow the way of goodness and uprightness; the author adds either that it will lead to life, or that the way of wickedness leads to death.

TO THINK ABOUT

There are a number of concepts here, and towards the end the exact words are not always clear. Take some time to read this passage again, and then pray with the psalmist:

'Lead me in your truth, and teach me,
for you are the God of my salvation;
for you I wait all day long.'
(Psalm 25:5)

A QUESTION *of* ATTITUDE

'Discipline' here (v. 1) is probably used in the sense of learning, so we are taken back to the parental advice of chapters 1—9. The wise not only accept it but love it—they are teachable. The 'scoffers', on the other hand—the hardest cases of all, insolent and arrogant (see 1:22; 9:7)—refuse any kind of guidance or correction, and are impervious to reproof. Answering back is certainly not encouraged in this society!

Words and actions

Words have a lasting effect (v. 2): they 'bear fruit' because they are remembered. So good words can be a source of happiness to the speakers as well as to the hearers. On the other hand, the treacherous positively enjoy their violent actions.

Discretion is again urged (v. 3). Those who do not think before they speak, whether it is to give a promise, express an opinion or share information, will eventually say something which at best will give offence, and at worst may land the speaker in serious financial, social, physical or spiritual trouble. Amen-em-opet advises, 'Sleep a night before speaking.' Verse 5, like verse 3, contrasts those who hate deception, whether in words or actions, with those whose behaviour (and presumably what they say) is scandalous. The New Testament emphasizes the importance of truth and its effect not only on ourselves but on others: 'Putting away falsehood, let all of us speak the truth to our neighbours, for we are members of one another' (Ephesians 4:25).

Laziness and diligence

Our old acquaintance the lazybones (v. 4) will not begin anything (6:9–10), will not finish anything (12:27), and ends up restless and dissatisfied. The diligent, on the other hand (see also 10:4), can expect to see some profit from their efforts.

Obedience and rebellion

Righteousness and sin sound almost like people in verse 6; the one stands for conformity to God's law, the other for disobedience to it. Here, the consequences of choosing one or the other follow naturally, unlike in 12:2, where the results of human conduct are seen as due to divine intervention.

Appearances can be deceptive

Verse 7 has been interpreted as meaning that real wealth does not consist of worldly goods, so those who think themselves poor are actually rich, and vice versa. However, the more likely meaning is simpler: there is a perverseness in human nature which makes us conceal our true circumstances. In that case, this is simply an observation about people as the author sees them; no moral is pointed, and we are left to draw our own conclusions.

Poverty has its compensations

Although at first sight verse 8 seems to be saying that there is safety in wealth, a close reading seems to agree with Moffatt's translation:

A rich man may buy off his life;
a poor man can ignore the robber's threat.

There is something to be said for having few or no worldly goods to lose!

PRAYER

Lord, show me how to make wise choices. Help me to be
contented with my lot in life, but never lazy or complacent.
And may I remember that what I say and do affects other people
as well as myself.

A FUTURE, BRIGHT *or* DARK

'Light' and 'lamp' (v. 9) symbolize life, happiness and prosperity. The idea may come from the lamp in the temple of Jerusalem, always kept alight as a symbol of the presence of God with his people. Or it may mean the Law, as in:

> Your word is a lamp to my feet
>   and a light to my path (Psalm 119:105).

Either way, God's presence and God's word bring joy and life to the righteous, but those without it soon face the darkness of death.

Pride and humility (v. 10) is a familiar theme, but here, as well as bringing eventual humiliation (see 11:2), pride is an ingredient in every quarrel—not necessarily in a genuine difference of opinion, but in the sort of clash which comes between unyielding personalities. Nor will pride take correction, whereas humility listens to others and has the benefit of their opinions. The REB has 'Wisdom is found among friends in council', which has something in common with our 'Two heads are better than one'.

'Easy come, easy go' sums up verse 11, which gives a comforting word to those who have little means and few expectations. It is not clear whether the 'wealth hastily gotten' has been earned honestly or acquired dubiously ('hastily' is literally 'from vanity', or 'from nothing'). The moral, if there is one, is that wealth easily come by is often undervalued and frittered away; there is really nothing to beat hard work.

Human nature

In an observation on human psychology (v. 12), 'deferred' means 'long drawn out', not any change in what was originally promised. The 'tree of life' (see 3:18; 11:30) is used here not in a moral or spiritual sense, but to describe the boost to the drooping spirits when hopes are at last fulfilled. The early Church knew about hope deferred; they are exhorted: 'Be patient, therefore, beloved, until the ocming of the Lord... Strengthen your hearts, for the coming of the Lord is near' (James 5:7, 8).

The importance of taking advice is again stressed in verses 13 and 14, but in verse 13 there is something new. Unusually for Proverbs, the 'advice' is not simply common sense, but 'word' and 'commandment'—terms used for God's law. In a rare moment, the author reminds us that underneath all the practicalities of the book is the belief that faith is revealed by God, and not something we can work out for ourselves.

Verse 14 is about teaching from spiritual experience rather than by divine command, though the two are in harmony. It contains all that is life and health-giving (see 10:11), and offers an escape from Sheol, which waits to entrap and swallow its victims (see 1:12).

'Good sense' (v. 15) is one of the words for Wisdom, and this is about practical wisdom, the *savoir faire* which deals courteously and acceptably with any situation. The second half of the verse probably means that the indiscreet bring about their own downfall, although an alternative is 'the way of the faithless, or transgressors, is permanent'—that is, they are stuck with it and with themselves.

In verse 16, 'clever' means not intellectually brilliant, but sensible and perceptive. Those who have this sort of intelligence act appropriately with due regard to the circumstances. The foolish, by contrast, give themselves away by their unguarded speech.

What about the messenger?

One of the original tasks of Proverbs may have been to prepare future ambassadors for their duties, just as the *Teaching of Amen-em-opet* states its aim of enabling the pupil 'to return a report to one who has sent him'.

There was always the temptation to falsify messages for financial reward, so a great deal depended on the truthfulness and integrity of an envoy. The good ambassador does not mend the mistakes of the bad, but his words are helpful rather than unclear or untruthful.

PRAYER

Lord, there are some challenging ideas in this passage—reminders about pride, wealth and discretion and, above all, about the need to listen to you. Please help me to turn these thoughts into actions, and help me, too, to be a faithful witness to your truth at all times.

LISTENING *to* SOUND ADVICE

Whether it comes from parents, teachers, friends or business associates, good advice is essential if we are to succeed in life (v. 18). Many a ruined career comes from 'going it alone'. This verse summarizes the teaching of 1:10–33, which sets out the options in detail.

Our heart's desire

The first half of verse 19 repeats verse 12b, but expresses it more strongly. However, we must be sure that what we want so passionately is right; permanent satisfaction can only come from something worthwhile. There is a warning in the story of the Israelites in the desert, when '(God) gave them what they asked, but sent a wasting disease among them' (Psalm 106:15).

The second half of verse 19 makes a different but possibly related point. For the foolish, it is unthinkable to give up anything, however wrong.

'A friend in need is a friend indeed'

It is important to choose our friends carefully (v. 20), because the influence of one person on another is powerful. The extent to which other people mould our character is one of the themes of Proverbs (see, for example, 1:10; 2:12; 4:14). Paul gives the same warning, obviously quoting another popular saying: 'Do not be deceived: "Bad company ruins good morals"' (1 Corinthians 15:33).

However, this can work in reverse, if we follow the example of Jesus, who kept company with 'tax collectors and sinners' and whose influence was entirely good.

Inexorable consequences

'Misfortune' and 'prosperity' (v. 21) are uncompromising words; retribution is inevitable and absolute. But in verse 22 there is an exception. We might expect to read that the good have something to leave, and the wicked nothing, but in fact there are cases in which the sinner grows rich. Then justice comes at one remove—ill-gotten gains will eventually pass to the righteous, correcting the balance.

Verse 23 considers the matter of good management. The size of our resources is not important; the way in which we handle them is. The second line of this verse is not easy to connect with the first, unless we read with the KJV, 'But there is that (which) is destroyed for want of judgment'.

The question of 'Spare the rod, spoil the child?' is raised in verse 24. In the ancient Near East at this time, corporal punishment was regarded as essential to a child's education. Egyptian schoolboys were made to copy out, 'Boys... listen when they are beaten'.

However, this verse is making a much more general point—that spoiling children is a sign not of parental love but of its absence. In Proverbs there is a lot about loving and patient training and guidance (see 1:8–9; 4:8–9), and a grateful memory of one such godly home (4:3–4). But the Bible does not expect parents to be perfect. For example, Ephesians 6:4 warns that too much severity can be counter-productive: 'Fathers, do not provoke your children to anger; but bring them up in the discipline and instruction of the Lord.'

Nor can parents compel wisdom or be held responsible for their family members' lifestyles. The final choice is the children's, who bring either 'poverty and disgrace' or 'honour' on themselves and their parents.

Satisfaction promised

The bodily needs of the righteous are provided for; the wicked are likely to go hungry (v. 25).

This looks forward to Mary's words as she anticipates the birth of Jesus:

He has filled the hungry with good things,
   and sent the rich away empty (Luke 1:53).

TO THINK ABOUT

There are a number of ideas and a lot of advice here. Think about them, and ask God to show you which is the most important for you at this time. Then pray that he will teach you what he wants you to learn and remember.

41 PROVERBS 14:1-9

BUILDING PROSPERITY

'The wisdom of women' is the literal translation of 'the wise woman' (v. 1); but what does it mean? It may be an extension of 9:1, in which Wisdom is represented as a busy housewife. This verse enlarges on the qualities of the home-maker. The stability of the home depends on the woman's constructive wisdom. This thought is unusual in the ancient world; for this writer, a woman is not merely a chattel, but the making of, or, if she is foolish, the undoing of her husband. She is the builder not only of his happiness but of his prosperity.

The need for a life founded on reverent obedience to God (v. 2; see 1:7) is central to the whole thought of Proverbs. Those who have this relationship with him walk in integrity, with a clear sense of direction. To despise him need not be by words or even by intention; it can be unconscious. Every time we deviate from his way and obey our own judgment instead of his, we show contempt for him, whether we mean it or not.

The need for self-discipline and self-control is emphasized throughout this chapter. Verse 3 may be saying that when we speak foolishly we 'make a rod for our own back', because our words will rebound on us. Alternatively, 'rod' may mean a shoot, or twig, which would be saying that what comes out of our mouths is the product of what is in our hearts, just as a shoot comes from the stem of a tree (see 10:31). The message is that we damage ourselves by such talk; safety lies in prudence.

Truthfulness, as well as discretion, is advised in verse 5; this is yet another warning about the danger as well as the sin of committing perjury (see 6:19; 12:17).

Future success

A number of meanings for verse 4 have been suggested; the KJV has 'Where no oxen are, the crib is clean', which has been interpreted as saying that there must be a certain amount of upheaval and mess for any worthwhile work to go on. The thought is probably less complicated: the wise farmer knows that he must have oxen, and in good condition, if he is to plough his land. The kindness to animals which is implied here, unlike that in 12:10, is not for their sake, but is necessary for the well-being of the property and the family.

Verses 6 and 7 focus on wasted abilities and wasted time. The 'scoffers' are capable of thought, but do not care to use that ability (v. 6). Like the 'fools' of 1:7, the scoffers despise wisdom, and are too arrogant to accept instruction, so of course, unlike their opposites who understand because they want to, they make no headway in learning.

It follows that they have little to offer to others (v. 7). The sooner we get away from them, the better, because we shall get no worthwhile conversation out of them.

To be able to assess the present with a view to its future consequences, whether in terms of our careers or our conduct, is the essence of shrewdness (v. 8). The inability of the foolish to think realistically not only leads to self-deceit but misleads others.

Spiritual insolence

It is unusual for Proverbs to mention formal religion, and the 'guilt offering' (v. 9) was a specialized sacrifice, not one of the most usual, but confined to particular offences (see, for example, Leviticus 19:20–22). Either this is saying that the thoughtless have no time for sacrifices or for formal religion in general, or that they see guilt as a subject for mockery. The contrast is between the fools and their lack of concern about the damage they cause, and those who obey God and have a loving relationship with him.

TO THINK ABOUT

Those who are enlightened with the True Light... know very well that order and fitness are better than disorder, and therefore they choose to walk orderly. Therefore they are not in so great anxiety as the others.

Theologia Germanica, c. 1350

COMFORT & CHALLENGE

For all of us, there are some things, sad or joyful, which nobody else can share; they are too deeply felt to be discussed (v. 10). Sometimes, we hide our griefs behind a mask of happiness (v. 13). We look cheerful and composed, but to ourselves, we say like Job 'My heart faints within me' (Job 19:27). It is a comfort that in this loneliness we can say with the psalmist:

O Lord, you have searched me and known me.
You know when I sit down and when I rise up;
* you discern my thoughts from far away* (Psalm 139:1–2).

A reversal of fortune

In 12:7 it is the sturdily-built house of the righteous which survives; here in verse 11, the tent is more durable than the conventional dwelling. Perhaps this is a memory of an earlier nomadic age, when the tent was the centre of family life. Whatever the technicalities, the point is that the household of the upright will be preserved and (if we take 'flourish' literally) even be enhanced by God. It is not the building itself but the life inside it which matters.

Taking the wrong road

The traveller chooses what looks like the right (literally 'straight') road (v. 12) which will lead, and might even be a short cut, to the desired destination—presumably that of worldly success. However, too late it becomes apparent that it all ends in disaster. Once again the writer emphasizes the difficulty, yet the importance, of discriminating between the way of good and the way of evil, a theme which has run through Proverbs from the first chapters (see, for example, 1:15–16; 2:8).

Ultimate justice

There is a another possible way of interpreting verse 14's version of 'we get what we deserve'. The KJV reads, '…and a good man (shall be satisfied) from within himself'—that is, the good find reward in their inward experiences. However, this is out of line with the general thought of Proverbs, which deals in terms of outward recompense rather than inward satisfaction.

Folly and sense

Verses 15–17 draw to our attention three different ways of being a fool.

First, the 'simple', or gullible, take on trust what they should verify for themselves (v. 15). The REB has 'A simpleton believes every word he hears.'

Second, the over-confident 'throw off restraint' (literally 'pass beyond bounds') and become disastrously arrogant (v. 16).

Third, the hot-tempered act according to their feelings, and not according to the merits of the case (v. 17). At the same time, the cold calculation of the schemer can be even harder to live with. This verse has some affinity with 'Would you rather be a knave or a fool?'

Our choices, and our behaviour, described in verses 15–17, will not go unnoticed. The uninstructed and immature (see v. 18; also 1:22), if they continue in the same way, will end up looking fools; those who have been taught to use their judgment, the 'clever' in the sense of 'shrewd', will wear their knowledge as an ornament.

PRAYER

Thy way, not mine, O Lord,
However dark it be:
Lead me by Thine own hand,
choose out the path for me.
Not mine, not mine the choice
In things or great or small;
Be Thou my guide, my strength,
My wisdom and my all.

Horatius Bonar (1808–89)

GOODNESS ALWAYS WINS?

The picture of verse 19 belongs to the culture of the time: the inferior prostrating themselves before the superior, or waiting at the gate hoping for favours, as Jesus described in the parable of the rich man and Lazarus (Luke 16:20–21). The belief that moral goodness always triumphs in this life persisted in the face of all evidence to the contrary until the Wisdom of Solomon proposed the doctrine of rewards and punishments after death: 'Men will see the wise man's end, without understanding what the Lord has purposed for him and why he took him into safe keeping… but it is they whom the Lord will laugh to scorn' (Wisdom 4:17–18, NEB).

The comment that it is easier for the rich to have friends than it is for the poor (v. 20) is an observation about human nature; the moral teaching comes in verse 21. Unkindness to the underprivileged, especially to our 'neighbours'—those close to us, to whom we owe special sympathy—is not only foolish (see 11:12), but sinful. Contempt spells rejection of the will of God; kindness brings the joy of his blessing.

The question form (v. 22) is rare in Proverbs; it is used to make sure we know the answer. We are urged to avoid making evil plans—always a mistake and a wrong activity. By contrast, good intentions towards others bring loyal friends. 'Loyalty and faithfulness' are words used to describe God's character (see 3:3). 'Loyalty' is often translated 'faithful love', the love which Jesus showed to his disciples when, 'having loved his own who were in the world, he loved them to the end' (John 13:1).

'Faithfulness' means reliability and stability. Here, both are used of human relationships; they are the response we can at least hope for if we first offer them.

Verse 23 argues that deeds, not words, produce results. Proverbs has no time for indolence (see 6:6–11); it praises work as the means of legitimate gain. Elsewhere the power of words is stressed; these passages provide a counterbalance.

Wealth and truth

In verse 24, the choice is between the 'crown' of the wise and the 'garland' of the fool. Our wisdom and foolishness cannot be hidden, but show themselves in our way of life. However, for 'wisdom' we may read 'wealth', which would mean that wisdom brings success in life, but the only reward of the stupid is their own folly. Against this interpretation is the fact that wealth is usually thought of as a gift from wisdom (3:16; 8:18), not as an ornament beautifying the wise.

The advisability of speaking the truth in a court of law, and the inadvisability and wrongness of perjury, have already been mentioned (6:19; 12:17). Verse 25 goes a step further. Honesty is not only right, it can save someone unjustly accused from death. False testimony deceives the judge and the public, and can bring ruin on an innocent victim. This is an important reminder to those living in a legal system where verdicts largely depended on witnesses.

The fear of the Lord

Living our lives with reverent regard to God's law gives a sense of safety and security for ourselves and our families (v. 26). Like the 'teaching of the wise' (13:14), from which this godly life develops, it also is a constant source of refreshment and delight, and saves us from the 'snare' of ungodliness, which brings fear, pain and destruction (v. 27).

PRAYER

Thank you, Lord, for your promises of safety and joy. Help me always to remember them, and may I show your faithfulness and loyalty in all my dealings with others.

TRUE GLORY

Although the king in Proverbs is not a constitutional monarch, he cannot rule without the support of his people. Solitary splendour leads nowhere (v. 28), and this applies at every level. We need each other if we are to operate effectively.

Verses 29 and 30 show that thinking hard before speaking angrily is a mark of good sense; thoughtfulness and self-control contribute to peace of mind. On the other hand, to lose our temper 'exalts' folly—literally 'lifts it up' for everyone to see—and does nobody any good.

Our attitudes affect us physically as well as emotionally, a fact well known to modern medicine (v. 30). A tranquil mind—'a heart of healing'—is life-enhancing, while 'passion', which can mean both anger and jealousy (the root of the word is 'red', that is, whatever inflames us), when it is unresolved, is correspondingly destructive to our 'bones', that is, our whole frame.

Creation and Creator

There is nothing new in the concern shown in verse 31 about our treatment of the poor and oppressed. What is new is the reason for this concern. We are all created by God; Job, speaking about his slaves, asks:

Did not he who made me in the womb make them?
 And did not one fashion us in the womb? (Job 31:15).

So it follows that our behaviour towards each other reflects our attitude to God. Jesus says, 'Just as you did it to one of the least of these who are members of my family, you did it to me' (Matthew 25:40). There is an obligation on God's people to care for the poor, and to fight their cause.

The meaning of the first part of verse 32 is clear. Evil deeds bring evil consequences. In the second part, the NRSV follows the Greek Old Testament, which contrasts the refuge of integrity with the ruin brought about by wickedness. Alternatively, the KJV reads with the Hebrew, 'The righteous hath hope in his death', presumably feeling the way towards a positive attitude to death expressed by the psalmist:

Into your hand I commit my spirit;
you have redeemed me, O Lord, faithful God (Psalm 31:5).

However, that is not in line with the thought of Proverbs, which regards death as the ultimate calamity.

Private and public life

Verse 33 at first seems to state the obvious: we would expect Wisdom to be a welcome guest with the discerning, but a stranger to the foolish. However, once again, if the Hebrew text is followed we are told that Wisdom is also known 'in the midst of fools'. 'Fools' here are the simple and untaught; it could be that even among them, Wisdom does not go entirely unrecognized.

Verse 34 echoes the teaching of the prophets. For them, national success comes not through skilful tactics but by obedience to God's word—an uncompromising test borne out by history (see Amos 1—2). Prosperity, power and reputation result from following the divine law, but national sin brings disgrace—a strong word used only here and in Leviticus 20:17. Integrity in a nation is as essential as it is in the individual.

The same is true at the personal level (v. 35). 'Servant' means any official of any rank; whoever they are, it is not good luck or favouritism but their own right dealings or shortcomings that determine their standing with the king.

PRAYER

Direct this and every nation in the ways of justice and of peace;
that we may honour one another, and seek the common good.

From Order for Holy Communion (Rite 'A'),
Alternative Service Book 1980

45 PROVERBS 15:1-9

Speaking *of* Speech

Verses 1, 2, 4, 5 and 7 are about talking and listening.

Verse 1 is probably one of the best-known sayings of Proverbs. The 'soft' answer is not weak, but calm; taking the steam out of a situation, and encouraging sensible discussion. This sort of restraint was an essential qualification for a courtier or a diplomat. By contrast, it only takes one harsh word to cause vexation and pain.

Verse 2 contrasts the judicious speech of the wise, dispensed (literally 'measured out') at appropriate times and in appropriate quantities, with the torrent of foolish words poured out by those who have nothing worthwhile to say, but who delight in saying it.

In verse 4, we are reminded of the life-giving or death-dealing effect of words. A gentle, literally 'healing', tongue can be life-enhancing and life-preserving (see 13:12), but cruel, untrue and twisted words have a devastating effect on morale.

Verse 5 is about listening to other people's words: 'instruction', 'admonition' and 'prudence' take us back to the parents' teaching (see 1:1–7). It is never too late to learn, and if we are wise we value truth enough to pay the price for it. Fools are not necessarily stupid, but do not have any serious wish to become better people, an attitude which encourages arrogance and prevents learning.

In verse 7, 'lips' and 'minds' go together, since what we speak is the product of what we think. It is salutary to be reminded how much influence for good or bad our words have.

God takes note

'Keeping watch' (v. 3) commonly describes the watchmen of a city (see 2 Kings 9:17); the idea that God sees and knows everything is not necessarily a negative one. 2 Chronicles 16:9 says, 'The eyes of the Lord range throughout the entire earth, to strengthen those whose heart is true to him.'

Nor is this a matter of 'Big Brother is watching you'. God's knowledge has a purpose: he can foresee the consequences of our chosen lifestyle. So verse 6 points out that by our actions we can store up good, or bring trouble on ourselves and on others because we eventually lose what we have gained by deceitful or unjust means.

Hateful or pleasing to God?

Verse 8 is one of the few references to sacrifice in Proverbs (see 7:14; 14:9). It is also, like 14:34, one of the times when 'the wise' speak out in open agreement with the prophets. Sacrifice itself is not condemned, but sacrifice without goodness is hypocrisy, and totally unacceptable to God (see Amos 5:22). On the other hand, the prayer of the righteous gives him pleasure. Sacrifice and prayer are not exact equivalents, perhaps because sacrifice is an outward act which anyone, sincere or insincere, can perform, whereas the prayer of the individual is private and more likely to be heartfelt.

Verse 9 makes the same contrast, but refers to moral conduct rather than religious observance. No doubt the two verses are connected, because behaviour is the outward sign of faith or unbelief.

TO THINK ABOUT

*What we say has the power to bring calm instead of quarrelling,
and life instead of misery. We must never underestimate
the power of words.*

PRAYER

*Lord, be the guardian of my speech,
and let my actions be pleasing to you.*

DISCIPLINE & DEATH

There seems to be a progression in verse 10. The wayward, who leave the 'way of righteousness', are severely disciplined, but those who refuse reproof are asking for death. Alternatively, the 'severe discipline' itself may be death, in which case this is saying that a wilfully and persistently undisciplined life will lead to either an early or a violent death. Whichever interpretation we prefer, the message is that it is wise as well as right to accept correction.

And after death (v. 11)? Sheol and Abaddon (from the root 'to perish') both mean the place of the departed; in Revelation 9:11, 'Abbadon' is the name of the angel of the abyss, who sends souls to Sheol. This verse represents an advance in thinking about life after death: unlike some other passages in the Old Testament (for example, Psalm 88:10–12), where it seems that God has nothing to do with the world of the dead, it declares that he knows what goes on there just as much as he knows about what happens on earth (see v. 3). The same point is made by Job, who declares:

> Sheol is naked before God,
> and Abaddon has no covering (Job 26:6).

The 'scoffers' are the hardest cases (v. 12); they not only hate reproof like all the rest of us, but they have no intention of learning, from teachers, parents, or anybody else. No way forward is suggested for them, because they do not want it.

The 'heart' (v. 13) represents all our thoughts and attitudes, shown in the way we look. It is our mind-set which lifts or crushes the spirit, not our circumstances, which are not even mentioned here. This is an observation on life as it is, without any particular moral teaching.

Verse 14 argues that both knowledge and folly create an appetite for more, but people go about satisfying their desires in different ways. Those who really long for wisdom take trouble; the foolish and empty-headed 'graze' (the term used for animals) without any real sense of purpose.

True riches

The three sayings in verses 15–17 do not condemn wealth as such, but they remind us that it does not automatically bring happiness. It may have been gained unfairly and leave a bitter taste in our mouths; it may become the be-all and end-all of our lives, and leave us in the end with nothing. It is certainly useless unless we are at peace with ourselves and with others.

Verse 15 says that life is what you make it. Just as our attitudes colour our personalities (v. 13), they also colour our whole experience. In both verses it is not our circumstances but our mind-set which affects the way we live our lives. 'A cheerful heart' is literally 'a good heart'; if we are in good heart, even when things are a struggle we shall always find something in which we can take pleasure.

Verse 16 identifies the great requirement for contentment—the 'fear of the Lord'. There is no comparison between a godly life, even when there is little in the way of material goods and possessions, and wealth, if it is accompanied by 'trouble'—literally turmoil, confusion, perplexity. 'There is great gain in godliness combined with contentment' (1 Timothy 6:6).

Verse 17, another much-quoted saying, is not about favouring a vegetarian diet, but remarks the obvious—that a simple meal prepared and eaten with affection is better than an elaborate feast where there is ill-feeling. A 'fatted ox' represents great luxury, but does not guarantee that the celebration will be a success, as the father of the prodigal son found when he killed the fatted calf for the returned sinner and incurred the wrath of the elder brother (Luke 15:25–30).

TO THINK ABOUT

Ten thousand, thousand precious gifts
My daily thanks employ;
Nor is the least a cheerful heart,
That tastes those gifts with joy.

Joseph Addison (1672–1719)

PATIENCE & HARD WORK

Both patience and hard work have good consequences, just as their opposites bring disaster. 'Hot-tempered' (v. 18) does not mean one who is angry, but one who makes a habit of losing his or her temper. Contrasted is the calm, considered reaction of the person who takes time to think before responding to a situation. Since most quarrels depend more on people than on the ideas or events about which they disagree, self-control or the lack of it usually tips the balance towards or away from an unpleasant falling-out.

The 'lazybones' meets with obstacles at every turn, and makes no progress, probably because there is no will to do so (v. 19). The upright, on the other hand, are honest and straightforward, and their path is carefully constructed, literally 'cast up' in the sense of made level by casting up the earth and removing obstacles (see Isaiah 40:3).

The rebellious offspring (v. 20) are as foolish as the lazy and hot-tempered. ('Foolish' here means literally 'fool of a man', with the same sense as 'wild ass of a man' in Genesis 16:12.) The first part of this verse, about the joy which a wise child brings, is the same as 10:1, but the second, instead of remarking on the grief which folly brings to a mother, gives an example of what happens all too often between parents and children, especially in adolescence. There is no need to spell out how hurtful it is for a parent to be the object of their child's contempt.

In verse 21, folly has a moral as well as an intellectual meaning. We are tempted to ask, 'How can anyone enjoy being a fool?' The answer is that fools cannot or will not understand what is good or bad, and so have no idea that sin will bring unhappy consequences. A person with insight, on the other hand, understands the laws which govern life, and acts in a wise, upright, straightforward way. According to this verse our attitude to Wisdom—whether we desire or reject her—forms the basis of our character.

More advice is better

'Counsel', or consultation (see 11:14), is desirable in family, business, social and public affairs. Without it, things are more likely to go wrong (literally 'be broken') (v. 22). We might think that we can have too much advice, but the author clearly believes that the more opinions we canvass, the better.

There is, by contrast, no doubt about the value of the 'apt answer'—not necessarily the answer to a question, but words in general (v. 23). A well-considered, appropriate word which is relevant to the situation ('a word in season' is literally 'a word in its time') brings joy both to the one who speaks and the one who receives it. 'How good it is!' means 'How effective and useful it is!'

Upwards or downwards?

Verse 24 adds another thought to the theme of the 'two ways' which recurs throughout Proverbs. The way of evil leads down to Sheol—the place of the dead. On the other hand, the way of goodness leads upwards. If this means the way to heaven, it represents an advance in thinking about life after death, since up to now Sheol has been the destination of all those who die, good and bad alike. However, 'upwards' may equally well mean 'above ground'—that is, the righteous enjoy a long life, while the wicked are on the path to an early death.

Justice for the poor

Social injustice is present, but it will not be allowed to go unchecked (v. 25). The house of the 'proud', that is, of anyone unscrupulous, has often been acquired by appropriating the property of the poor, among whom widows are especially vulnerable. The Wisdom literature of the ancient Near East condemns the crime of moving or removing 'boundary stones', the marks of legal ownership of land, and the prophets also warn that such crimes will be punished (see Isaiah 5:8–10). However, this is only an example; all kinds of exploitation are condemned. In 14:31, we are reminded of our duty to respect the underprivileged who are, like us, part of God's creation. Here, the thought is developed, and God's own intervention on their behalf is envisaged.

PRAYER

Lord, give me a true understanding of what life is about, and of how you want me to live it. Keep me from the sins of folly and pride and greed, and help me to follow your upward path.

THINKING & SPEAKING

What we plan, and the words that we speak as the result of our plans, can, like the Old Testament sacrifices, be either 'pure' or 'unclean'—acceptable or unacceptable to God (v. 26). Ideas and words cannot be separated. Jesus says, 'Out of the abundance of the heart the mouth speaks' (Matthew 12:34).

Verse 28 contrasts the words that are the result of quiet meditation with the deluge of presumably unconsidered words which are also evil. The point is the same as that made in verse 2, with the addition of wisdom and folly being identified with goodness and wickedness.

Bribery and corruption

Bribery was universally condemned in the ancient Near East, and was equally universally practised. The picture here in verse 27 is of a householder responsible for providing a living for the family. Neither making a profit nor taking gifts need be wrong, but if the profit is made by injustice and greed, and if the gifts are taken as bribes, the home is disturbed and tense ('trouble' is the same word as in verse 6), because its values have become confused. By contrast, the household which does not practise bribery 'will live'—presumably meaning that they will enjoy a prosperous and harmonious family life.

Which prayers are heard?

God is 'far from', or inaccessible to, the wicked (see v. 8). They may pray, but their prayer will not be favourably received—they have chosen to be out of contact with God (v. 29). The possibility of their repenting is not mentioned, because as soon as they do so they become 'the righteous'—and are in communication with the Lord.

Good news

The meaning of 'the light of the eyes' (REB 'a bright look') in verse 30 is not altogether clear, but probably it describes the cheerful face of a friend. If so, the two parts of this proverb are about the heart-warming effect that those who bring good news have on those who receive it and on themselves.

Learning about learning

Wisdom's teaching is never flattering! 'Admonition' and arduous 'instruction' ('discipline') are a continuing process and a lifetime's project. But their benefits are proportionally great: 'wholesome admonition' (v. 31), literally 'the admonition of life', is the key to a place among those who are wise. 'To lodge' can mean 'to pass the night', but is used in poetry to express a permanent dwelling:

> You who live in the shelter of the Most High,
>   who abide in the shadow of the Almighty... (Psalm 91:1).

On the other hand, those who 'ignore' discipline, or 'treat it as of small value', also treat themselves as of little account, and so suffer from low self-esteem, while those who submit to correction find that the gain is all theirs (v. 32).

In verse 33, the fear of the Lord is not only the beginning of Wisdom (see 1:7), it is ongoing as we advance in learning. From first to last, reverent obedience to God guides us and teaches us the truth as we go through life. The last part of the verse reminds us that humility towards correction and instruction is necessary before we are rewarded with honour.

TO THINK ABOUT

In these verses, God is consistent in character and certain in guidance, so that we can say with the psalmist:

> *'You are indeed my rock and my fortress;*
> *for your name's sake lead me and guide me.'*
>   *(Psalm 31:3)*

GOD *is in* CHARGE

Up to now, God has most frequently appeared in the phrase 'the fear of the Lord'; from here onwards there is much more direct reference to him.

This passage is about his control over human life, and he is mentioned in every verse except verse 8. His power is described in a number of ways—some of them requiring rather a lot of faith if we are to accept them!

We propose, God disposes

For all our freedom to plan, we can only act in so far as God allows. In verse 1, our thoughts and preparations are contradicted by God's word; in verse 9, they are directed by him. The belief in God's absolute control of human affairs is strong in the Old and New Testaments: 'It depends not on human will or exertion, but on God who shows mercy' (Romans 9:16).

Usually, we do what seems right at the time (v. 2), but, ignorant and prejudiced as we are, we can only test the outcome by submitting our ways—our natures with their motives and their aims—to God's judgment. His verdict will be true and just, because he alone fully understands us. However, relief from anxiety is offered if we commit our activities and plans to his scrutiny.

Everything created fits into God's pattern; ultimately there will be no loose ends, because all will be treated appropriately (v. 4). The problem with this verse is the idea that God actually made the wicked with their deserved destruction in mind.

The sovereignty of God is absolute in the Old Testament, so this argument may be an attempt to answer the question, 'Why did God make the wicked?'—a problem which is addressed in the book of Job. Whatever the purpose of the life of the wicked, their ultimate fate is not in question (v. 5). Depend on it ('hand to hand'; see 11:21), the arrogant will be judged. 'The arrogant' are singled out in Proverbs for condemnation. Pride is the first of the seven things which God hates (6:17), and the proud will be punished along with the adulterers (6:29) and the perjurers (19:5), whom they have no idea they resemble.

How to make good

'Atoned for' (v. 6) usually refers to the removal of sin by means of sacrifice. Here, sin is dealt with not by sacrifice but by a life of loyalty and faithfulness and of reverent submission to God. It is assumed that we have repented; but repentance only makes sense if it brings a change in our ways. The prophets' teaching is the same: for example, 'When the wicked turn away from the wickedness they have committed and do what is lawful and right, they shall save their life' (Ezekiel 18:27).

The 'enemies' in verse 7 are personal, not national, enemies, but this is not a blanket promise that the righteous will never have any enemies. Jesus warns, 'If the world hates you, be aware that it hated me before it hated you' (John 15:18). Rather, this is to encourage us to please God in preference to other people. If we consult his wishes, we can be assured that he can handle the people we fear.

Part of pleasing God is that we must be honest at all costs. Verse 8 states in absolute moral terms what 15:16 promises in terms of well-being and happiness.

TO THINK ABOUT

Who fathoms the eternal thought?
Who talks of scheme and plan?
The Lord is God! He heedeth not
The poor device of man.
I know not what the future hath
Of marvel or surprise,
Assured alone that life and death
His mercy underlies.

John Greenleaf Whittier (1807–92)

KINGS & RULERS

The king of Israel is God's anointed, and rules as God's vice-regent. This is not suggesting that 'the king can do no wrong'; in the Law, he is warned that he must rule 'neither exalting himself above other members of the community nor turning aside from the commandment' (Deuteronomy 17:20).

The prophets also were not afraid to challenge the monarch: Nathan's rebuke to David (2 Samuel 12:1–15) and Elijah's long-running battle with Ahab (1 Kings 17:1–7; 18; 21) are examples.

Proverbs approves of monarchy as a principle but, like the prophets, recognizes that the king himself can be corrupt, or even incapable of ruling wisely (29:12).

Oriental kings had absolute power, and sometimes were worshipped as gods. None of this is available to the kings of the Old Testament: God is the supreme king, and authority is delegated by him. The 'royal' psalms make the point; for example:

The Lord is king...
The Lord is great in Zion;
  he is exalted over all the peoples (Psalm 99:1–2).

These verses, with the exception of 11, are about what is expected of the king. Whether they were written during the monarchy, or whether they are of later origin, when Judea was ruled by various princes during the Greek period, the ideas are the same. This is how a king should be.

Words and decisions

'Inspired decisions' (literally 'divination') (v. 10) suggests that the king must have divinely inspired powers of judgment bordering on the supernatural. The 'wise woman', in conversation with David, says, 'My lord has wisdom like the wisdom of the angel of God, to know all things that are on the earth' (2 Samuel 14:20).

Given that God is the source of this wisdom, the true king will make just decisions.

The king must have a good conscience (v. 12), and must recognize truth in others (v. 13). Just as 'righteousness exalts a nation' (14:34), so the throne depends on it. He must detest the wrong and rejoice in the right. 'Abomination' and 'delight', feelings often attributed to God, must be shared by his earthly representative.

The king's power

Although Israelite kings are not above the law, in practice they have the powers of life and death in their hands (v. 14). In a single chapter, Solomon arranges the political assassinations of his half-brother Adonijah (1 Kings 2:25), his father's former army commander Joab (1 Kings 2:29–34), and the traitor Shimei (1 Kings 2:46). So courtiers do well to remember that their careers, and even their lives, depend on the king's pleasure, and it is wise to 'appease' him—an expression meaning to 'cover' or pacify his wrath. Conversely, the king's favour is as welcome and gracious as the rain which is needed for the ripening crops (v. 15).

Positive justice is the subject of verse 11. The king is not mentioned, but we presume that honesty is a feature of his reign. 2 Samuel 14:26 mentions weighing 'by the king's weight', which suggests that some weights and measures were given royal authority. Here, the authorization is taken back to God himself: just as he hates false weights and measures (11:1), he promotes fair and correct ones.

TO THINK ABOUT

This is not only about long-ago monarchs, it applies to anyone who has authority over others. Sometimes we forget what power we have over other people. Fairness, justice and integrity are required, however small or great are our responsibilities.

BETTER *than* GOLD & SILVER

The comparison in verse 16 is common in Wisdom literature (see, for example, 3:13–18). It is not implying that there is anything wrong in itself with wealth, provided it is honestly gained, but the rewards of getting wisdom and understanding (some effort is implied here) are far greater, as well as longer-lasting.

How to avoid trouble

Verse 17 has two possible meanings. If 'evil' means 'misfortune', it is saying that integrity smoothes our path and protects us. The path of the upright is free from obstacles. If it means 'wickedness', it is saying that by keeping on a straight course we guard our whole being from the corruption of sin (see 11:3).

The English proverb 'Pride goes before a fall' probably comes from verse 18. There is an Egyptian saying: 'Pride and arrogance are the destruction of their master.'

Pride is particularly evil. It is in opposition to the great principle of wisdom, 'the fear of the Lord'. The proud are at odds with themselves (8:36), with their neighbours (13:10), and worst of all with God (16:5). In the end, pride brings disaster which can come from any direction and in a number of ways ('destruction' can mean crushing, breaking, or crashing).

In verse 19, 'divide the spoil' is a military term, referring here to a gang of criminals taking something by violence, and sharing it between them. It is better to be 'lowly', or unassuming, even if there is no profit in it, than to associate with the 'proud', or the oppressive and over-bearing, and to share in their ill-gotten gains.

The key to happiness

'Attentive to a matter' (v. 20) can be understood in more than one way. It may mean something like business acumen, or, if we translate 'matter' literally as 'word', it may be saying that listening to good advice is a good idea. But sometimes 'word' means 'the Word'—that is, God's Word, which at the time when Proverbs was edited would mean the Law and possibly the Prophets. In that case the two halves of the verse tell us that obedience to the Word will bring prosperity and satisfaction.

The 'wise of heart' (meaning 'of mind') are 'called'—or given credit for being—perceptive (v. 21). When God says to Solomon, 'Ask what I should give you', Solomon replies, 'An understanding mind… able to discern between good and evil' (1 Kings 3:5, 9). This is the beginning of Solomon's reputation for wisdom.

Discernment shows itself in appropriate speech, which is persuasive, or effective, because it is founded on a right assessment of a person or situation (v. 23). Such words are likely to be pleasant and friendly (v. 24) but they need not be calculating. Spoken at the right time, they can have a beneficial and revitalizing effect both mentally and physically on the hearers—like God's words, which are:

Sweeter also than honey,
*   and drippings of the honeycomb* (Psalm 19:10).

This is good advice for everyone, but especially for those teachers, sometimes addressed in Proverbs, who are training students for positions where they will need gifts of diplomatic persuasion.

Living with ourselves

We have already encountered the idea of wise words and godly lives as 'fountains of life' (10:11; 13:14; 14:27). In verse 22, wisdom, or good sense, itself brings the same benefits to us. However, folly, the opposite, brings the opposite result. Our punishment is to have 'made a rod for our own back'.

TO THINK ABOUT
Let your speech always be gracious, seasoned with salt,
so that you may know how you ought to answer everyone.
(Colossians 4:6)

52

WORKING & PLANNING

Verse 25 is the same as 14:12—a reminder to us to think carefully about right and wrong before we make choices which affect our way of life.

Verse 26 states a hard fact—that we are driven by the need to work; not in this case for the sake of job satisfaction ('work' here means 'toil' or 'drudgery', hardly enjoyable words) but because we have to eat. The work ethic is strong not only in Proverbs but throughout the Bible. Paul says to the early Church, 'Anyone unwilling to work should not eat' (2 Thessalonians 3:10).

Perhaps this verse is the forerunner of our 'Hunger is the best sauce'.

Mischief-making

Lies, abuse (v. 27), gossip or mere whispers (v. 28), tough manipulation (v. 29) and non-verbal communication (v. 30) are all ways of spreading damage. The 'scoundrel' is the person of little worth (see 6:12), who invents (literally 'digs up') scandal and whose speech burns into its victims (v. 27). The perverse, or false (see 2:12), by their whispered insinuations can alienate friends. The violent forcibly encourage their associates into undesirable ways. Perhaps worst of all are the unspoken signs of malice—the subtle mannerisms conveying unpleasant messages (see 6:13)—which communicate a wealth of meaning without a word being spoken. We need to be on our guard against all these things, in ourselves and in others.

Age and reward

The thought behind verse 31 is that since, according to Proverbs, a long life is promised to the righteous, old age is not only God's reward for right living but has a beauty of its own. The elderly wicked do not figure, since they do not exist, having been cut off before their time!

The power of self-control

'One who captures a city' (v. 32) refers to military success, which then as now tends to steal the limelight from quieter exploits, and particularly from the achievements of those who are being trained in diplomatic skills. However, patience and self-discipline are equally if not more difficult than victory in battle, and in the end more deserving of praise, because we have to fight not an external enemy but ourselves (see 14:29).

God, not chance, decides

The casting of lots, common in the ancient world, was used from time to time in Israel to find out what God wanted (see, for example, Leviticus 16:8; 1 Samuel 14:41). The 'Urim and Thummim', used in this way, were thought to be stones worn by the high priest over his heart, which in some way gave positive or negative indications. The choosing by lot continues into the New Testament (see Acts 1:26, where Judas Iscariot's replacement is sought), but is never mentioned after Pentecost. The 'lap' here in verse 33 is the pocket-like fold in the robe into which the lots are thrown, and from which one is picked out.

TO THINK ABOUT

At the end of all this procedure, although we may think our fate is decided by chance or by ourselves, it is God who makes the final decision in the affairs of people and of nations. Paul reminds us:

'We know that all things work together for good for those who love God, who are called according to his purpose.'
(Romans 8:28)

53 PROVERBS 17:1-9

RELATIONSHIPS *of* MANY KINDS

These verses, which at first sight look unconnected, have running through them the theme of relationships—within families, with friends, with members of the household, with acquaintances of every kind, and with God.

The family is the setting for verses 1, 2 and 6. 'Feasting with strife' (v. 1) is literally 'sacrifice with strife'. After certain sacrifices, some of the meat was left to be eaten (see 7:14), and this formed the main dish of a feast. However, family celebrations are notoriously stressful! Then as now, such occasions could be noisy and exhausting, and quarrels were likely to arise. It is preferable to eat in peace, even if it means a simple meal, than to be at odds with each other, however elaborate the menu.

In verse 2, the virtues of hard work and the use of intelligence are once again praised. In ancient Israel, a slave was counted as one of the family, and could even become the heir if the master had no son (see Genesis 15:2–3). Where a child brings disgrace on the family, the clever, capable slave can displace that child as an heir after the father's death. The message here is that ability can outrun privilege, even in a social structure where privilege is well-established.

Since, according to Proverbs, long life is the reward for goodness and to have children is a blessing, to live to see our grandchildren (v. 6) brings a special joy—as many grandparents can testify. However, the relationships between the generations need to be good at every level. We approve of children being obedient and well disciplined—in other words, a credit to their parents. But here it is pointed out that parents also can, and should, bring pleasure and happiness to their children. Family relationships are two-way, and the happiest households are those where each generation is given the appropriate dignity and support.

Wicked talk

It is not only the person who spreads scandal who is guilty; those who listen are equally to blame. Taking notice of wicked talk implies that we are wicked (v. 4); welcoming lies makes us liars (literally 'a walking falsehood'). Evil words will die if they are not well-received, but they flourish in an atmosphere of approval.

Proverbs shows a special concern for the underprivileged. Mocking them (v. 5), like oppressing them, means we insult their—and our—Creator (see 14:31). To enjoy their misfortunes is a form of unkindness that will not go unnoticed or unpunished.

'Fine speech' (v. 7) means something excessive—what we sometimes call 'talking big'. The person who indulges in this is the worst kind of fool (the word appears only three times in Proverbs; here, in v. 21, and at 30:22). To a lack of moral, intellectual and spiritual insight is added an element of boorishness. In 1 Samuel 25:25, Abigail, whose husband is called Nabal, the same word as 'fool', says to David, 'Do not take seriously this ill-natured fellow, Nabal; for as his name is, so is he; Nabal is his name, and folly is with him.'

By contrast, the 'ruler', or 'noble person', has a title to be lived up to, so truthfulness is even more important.

If we want to keep our friends (v. 9), we have to forgive ('cover up' or ignore) hurtful words and thoughtless actions—easier said than done. But to dwell on these upsets does no good either to us or to the friendship.

Effective but wrong

Verse 8 is not about a close relationship, but about a practice which works like a magic stone, or amulet, for the one who offers it. The observation is made here without any moral comment, but elsewhere bribery is firmly forbidden, for example in Exodus 23:8.

How God sees us

Our relationships with each other are important and we must work at them. But does anyone ever fully know another human being? However we answer, God is the One from whom nothing is hidden (v. 3). Just as precious metals are refined by a physical process in order to reveal their true character, so God alone can make a true estimate of our strengths and weaknesses.

PRAYER

Lord, I need help in my relationships with other people,
but most of all I need to be right with you.

A MATTER *of* ATTITUDE

Some of us are more sensitive and responsive to reproof than others (v. 10). The wise person (literally, 'the one of discernment') will take it to heart and, presumably, act upon it. The fool, by contrast, has no wish to learn, cannot imagine having made a mistake, and cannot or will not recognize a rebuke even after being repeatedly hit on the head with it!

This is an observation about a type of person who appears in all cultures and at all times. Ahikar, an Assyrian writing in the seventh century bc, says, 'My son, smite a man with a wise word that it may be in his heart like a fever in summer; for if thou shouldest smite a fool with many rods, he will not perceive it.'

Because fools are stubborn and unteachable, once they get an idea nothing will change it, and this makes them a danger to themselves and others (v. 12). Meeting a bear robbed of her cubs means meeting ferocious anger; encountering a fool means encountering obstinacy and insensitivity.

Rebellion (v. 11) has no time for moderation of any kind, so the rebel will neither seek nor find any. We may ask whether this verse is about rebelling against God. However, since God is not mentioned, the 'cruel messenger' or 'messenger without mercy' is more likely to come as the consequence of political rebellion. For any courtier, such as the young men in training who are among the people to whom Proverbs is addressed, disloyalty to the regime means the death sentence.

This raises for us the issue of how far such loyalty is appropriate where a government is corrupt—not something with which Proverbs deals but which the prophets frequently have to face (see, for example, Isaiah 39:5–8). The whole question of civil disobedience is something which needs prayerful thought.

Reaping what we sow

The idea of the punishment fitting the crime is stated baldly, and without any qualification (v. 13). Those who do evil to others can expect trouble in their own lives—the appeal is basically to self-interest. Elsewhere, the spiritual aspect of retribution is stressed: it is the

Lord who punishes or rewards (10:3). A more positive way of treating each other is set out in 1 Peter 3:9: 'Do not repay evil for evil or abuse for abuse; but, on the contrary, repay with a blessing.'

The consequences of letting a quarrel go unchecked are equally undesirable. It is like opening a sluice: once the process has begun we cannot direct or control it. The right thing to do is to stop the disagreement before it begins.

False justice

The language in verse 15 is that of the law. Dishonest judges are universally condemned in both the Law (Exodus 23:7) and the Prophets (Isaiah 5:23). The first half of the verse means 'one who makes the wicked right, and the right wicked'—a picture of turning good and bad upside down. This strong emphasis on justice in the Old Testament paves the way for New Testament's use of legal language when it teaches about justification, and helps us understand what Paul means when he writes, 'For no human being will be justified in his sight by deeds prescribed by the law, for through the law comes the knowledge of sin' (Romans 3:20).

PRAYER

O send Thy Spirit, Lord,
now unto me,
That he may touch my eyes,
and make me see;
Show me the truth concealed
within Thy word,
And in Thy book revealed
I see Thee, Lord.

Mary A. Lathbury (1841–1913)

55 PROVERBS 17:16–22

NOT *at* ANY PRICE

We do not know whether the official teachers of wisdom charged a fee (v. 16), but that is immaterial here. Fools may think that wisdom can be handed out over the counter, but the hard truth is that they are lacking not only in the ability but also in the attitude of mind and will needed to acquire it. The word 'wisdom' instead of 'learning' or 'knowledge' suggests that it is moral as well as intellectual skills which are beyond the fool.

True friends

We have already met the fair-weather friend in 14:20; here in verse 17 is the true friend, who loves and cares whatever the circumstances. In the same way, although things can go wrong in families, kinship should come into its own in hard times. No contrast is intended between the friend and the relative; when we are in trouble we see what family ties are for, and we find out who are our friends.

However, friendship must be combined with common sense (v. 18). The warnings in 6:1–5 are repeated briefly here. Rash promises are liable to be a snare to those who make them, and are unlikely to do any good to the recipients.

Sadly, there are people who positively relish wrongdoing, and inevitably also delight in quarrelling (v. 19). The second part of this verse is not obviously connected with the first; it reads literally 'whoever makes a high gate', indicating perhaps arrogance or perhaps inhospitality. Either way, there will be some kind of a crash (literally 'a breaking'), and it will not be the sort of calamity that the house-holder enjoys. So the meaning of the whole could be, 'Strife always goes with a rebellious nature, and destruction is sure to come to the proud and selfish.'

Verse 20 repeats one of the main themes in Proverbs. God hates twisted thinking and lying words (11:20), and life does not go well for those who indulge in these habits.

Disappointing children are the subject of verse 21. As a rule, the Old Testament takes the line that 'sons are indeed a heritage from the Lord, the fruit of the womb a reward' (Psalm 127:3). But here there is a note of sad reality. The two words for 'fool' are different: there is the dull, unwilling person, uninterested in matters intellectual, moral and spiritual; and worse still, there is the boor whom we met in verse 7. Parents cannot disown such children; that is their tragedy, recognized also in 10:1.

The best medicine

Like 14:30, verse 22 makes the connection between mind and body. A cheerful (NEB has 'merry') outlook contributes towards wholeness ('good medicine' means literally 'healing' or 'health'). On the other hand, a dejected, downcast nature affects us for the worse. 'Bones' represent our whole frame. They can be vigorous, fat, and full of marrow (3:8; 16:24), or feeble, dry and decaying. Our well-being is affected by choice as well as by temperament. We can opt for a positive outlook—for example, looking towards recovery from illness or loss. Or we can cast ourselves in the role of the perpetual victims of circumstances and of other people.

PRAYER

Lord, give me a cheerful heart and a contented spirit. Help me to guard against arrogance and quarrelsomeness. I thank you for the friends who mean so much to me. Teach me the love that 'does not rejoice in wrongdoing, but rejoices in the truth'.
(1 Corinthians 13:6)

56

SECRET DEALINGS

Bribery (see v. 8) is forbidden in the Old Testament. Here in verse 23, the underhand aspect of such transactions is emphasized—it adds to the wrongdoing. Proverbs takes a consistently strong line about this particular sin.

Concentration and inattention

Those who seek wisdom will do so wholeheartedly. The 'discerning person' (v. 24) has some understanding of the issues involved, and will take trouble to attain true and right standards—God's standards of conduct. Fools, on the other hand, lack insight and stability and have no idea of what perseverance means; they cannot and will not concentrate, but are distracted by anything and everything. As the New Testament letter of James points out, 'The doubter, being double-minded and unstable in every way, must not expect to receive anything from the Lord' (James 1:8).

More about the next generation

Verse 25 is a variation on 10:1; 15:20 and 17:21, but the words for 'grief' and 'bitterness', or 'vexation' and 'misery', are sharper than the 'trouble' of verse 21. There is no limit to the sadness which sons and daughters can knowingly or unknowingly inflict on their parents. Although Proverbs has a lot to say about the need for good parenting, it also consistently places responsibility for the children's actions on themselves.

Against abuse of the law

To fine the innocent (v. 26) is not right (literally 'proper'). 'Noble' in the second line is the same word as 'ruler' in verse 7, meaning not necessarily an aristocrat, but someone who is noble in spirit, and who does not deserve punishment. Those who administer justice bear a heavy responsibility. To abuse their powers is inexcusable.

Silence is golden

To be 'cool in spirit' (v. 27) means to see a situation calmly and clearly, and to show composure and self-control. The person who has these qualities thinks before speaking, and such self-restraint often allows tempers to cool (see 15:1). The last-mentioned and least-quoted fruit of the Spirit (Galatians 5:23) is self-control.

Verse 28 means either that silence hides folly, or that the fool who has the sense to keep quiet is no longer a complete fool.

The thoughts underlying these two verses are not confined to the Bible but appear in other ancient Wisdom literature. Ptah-hotep says, 'If you are silent it is better than the *tef-tef* (a rare and valuable) plant.' The ideas and people in these verses have appeared before, but something extra is added. The secrecy of bribes is identified as particularly wrong; the inability of the fool to concentrate is mentioned for the first time; the sadness which children can bring upon their parents is intensified; caution in speech, always a sign of wisdom, is a good idea even for the foolish.

TO THINK ABOUT

All these warnings are relevant to today's society. The same temptations, inadequacies and disappointments are part of daily life; the advisability of thinking before we speak still applies.

PRAYER

Lord, keep me from thinking that I have learnt all the lessons you want to teach me. Thank you because there is always something new in your Word.

57 PROVERBS 18:1-8

The DANGERS *of* ISOLATION

Verse 1 is not condemning people who have no family: 'lives alone' means 'keeps aloof', and is about being not merely unsociable but anti-social. This inevitably leads to an undue attachment to individual preferences, whether about ideas or lifestyle, and does not make for good relations with others. 'Showing contempt' is the same word as is used in 17:14 to describe a quarrel breaking out. This whole attitude smacks of arrogance, and is bound to be a cause of resentment and dissension.

In verse 2, the foolish, quite apart from having no pleasure in or feel for wisdom, delight in holding forth with their own opinions, which of course reflect ignorance and lack of thought. In 12:23 and 15:2 this ignorance is displayed noisily and ostentatiously.

A puzzle to work out

Is the contempt which comes with wickedness (v. 3) directed towards the wicked, or against other people by the wicked? Either meaning is possible, but unless we change the second half of the verse, the second seems the more likely.

Once again, in verse 4 two meanings are possible. If this verse is about the wise, it is saying that starting from the depths of their hearts and minds, words come as a fountain, a constant source of blessing (see 13:14). If, however, it is speaking in a general sense, it contrasts those who conceal their thoughts with those who are prepared to speak clearly, candidly and wisely.

Justice for everyone

The absolute necessity for legal justice is once again emphasized in verse 5 (see 17:26), with special emphasis on the need to avoid favouritism. To 'be partial' is 'to lift up the face of the guilty'—that is, to raise him up from the ground as a sign of favour:

How long will you judge unjustly
  and show partiality to the wicked? (Psalm 82:2)

Stupid talk and malicious gossip

The fools' thoughtless words bring discord upon themselves and everybody else (v. 6), and since they are lies, they merit severe punishment. Verse 7 repeats this thought, but concentrates on the damage done to the foolish rather than to the whole of society.

Scandal is all the more dangerous because we are given to enjoying it (v. 8). Tasty morsels of gossip, like the food we eat, are consumed with relish and are taken into our being: the 'inner parts of the body' are thought of as the seat of memory. When we reflect on what is good, of course this can be beneficial. Amen-em-opet tells his readers that his words should 'rest in the casket of your belly, that they may be a key to your heart'.

TO THINK ABOUT

This passage has a lot to say about what we do to other people by our attitudes, our behaviour and our words. It is all too easy, without meaning to do so, to treat others with silent contempt while we hold forth with our own opinions or with tasty morsels of gossip which can cause untold hurt and misunderstanding. Paul writes, 'We do not live to ourselves, and we do not die to ourselves.'
(Romans 14:7)

PRAYER

Lord, show me how to represent you in all my contacts with others.

The LAZY VANDAL

Laziness has already been condemned as inconvenient and danger-ous to everyone concerned (see 6:6–11; 10:4; 12:24; 13:4). Here in verse 9, however, the 'lazybones' is downright destructive—not in the sense of being a thief or a murderer, but as one who brings ruin and devastation simply by leaving work (probably meaning daily, bread-winning employment) undone. To neglect our work is a way of destroying it.

Finding security in life

In the Bible, the name stands for the person, expressing character and qualities. It is so important that a name matches its owner that some-times there is a change—for example, in Genesis 32:28 Jacob ('sup-planter') becomes Israel ('one who strives with God'). 'The name of the Lord' (v. 10) appears only here in Proverbs, but is often used else-where in the Old Testament. 'The Lord', or 'I AM WHO I AM', is the name by which God reveals himself to Israel (Exodus 3:14), and in which he lovingly cares for them. So we may run to this name—that is, to the one who protects—for safety (literally 'to be set on high') in time of trouble.

In verse 11, wealth is invoked as protection, at any rate in the minds of those who have it. We might take this as a contrast with verse 10, saying that this security is only in people's imagination. Or, since in Proverbs wealth is usually a desirable source of power, it may simply be making an observation with no praise or blame attached.

Once again we are reminded (v. 12) that pride is in conflict with the basic principle in Proverbs of 'the fear of the Lord', and leads to disaster (see 16:18–19). One sign of self-importance is jumping to hasty conclusions (v. 13). Other Wisdom books give the same advice; Ben Sirach writes:

> *Do not answer without first listening,*
> *and do not interrupt when another is speaking*
> (Ecclesiasticus 11:8, NEB).

Verse 14 is a more sombre version of 14:13 and 17:22, with the emphasis on the effect of 'sickness', here meaning any suffering, on the human spirit—our inner self, the source of courage and strength. If someone has given up hope, and sees no meaning or purpose in life, even the best that medicine can offer is often ineffective. There is no reference here to help from God, but we can set alongside these thoughts the words of Paul: 'I can do all things through (Christ) who strengthens me' (Philippians 4:13).

In verse 15, 'intelligent', or 'discerning', and 'wise' mean the same thing (see 1:5). We must seek knowledge using all our faculties—among them, our minds for reflection and our ears for hearing. The quest for wisdom means total commitment.

How to open doors

The 'gift' in verse 16, unlike that in 17:8, is not a personal present, nor is it a bribe, but it comes somewhere between the two. In its realistic way, Proverbs observes that a gift made to the powerful can give help, protection and access to those with influence. This was an accepted practice at the time; it had its dangers (see 15:27), but given with integrity, the gift was regarded as a courtesy intended to smooth relationships. Perhaps this verse has something in common with Jesus' parable of the unjust steward, in which shrewdness is commended: 'The children of this age are more shrewd in dealing with their own generation than are the children of light' (Luke 16:8).

TO THINK ABOUT

God is our refuge and strength,
a very present help in trouble.
(Psalm 46:1)

PRAYER

Lord, may I always seek my safety and find the source of my values
in your teaching.

QUARRELS & LAWSUITS

In an Israelite court of law (v. 17), the prosecution or the plaintiff spoke first, and would argue eloquently until the cross-examination for the defence threw a different light on the matter. There are always two sides to a story, and this is a reminder to listen to both before making any judgment. It is the third warning in this chapter against forming hasty opinions.

In verse 18, an alternative way of deciding a dispute is by drawing lots (see 16:33). This is the only time in the Old Testament that the use of the lot is suggested for this purpose; presumably it is the preferred method when everything else has failed. Once decided, however powerful the opponents, the decision is to be accepted.

The 'ally' in verse 19 means literally a 'brother'. The text is difficult to translate, but what is being said must be that the closer the relationship, the more bitter, and harder to resolve, is the dispute—a sad but unfortunately true comment on what can happen among families and friends.

By describing their opposites, these three verses urge restraint, generosity and forbearance.

Eating our words

Our words make us what we are—in that sense we feed on them, and may be well-satisfied (v. 20, see also 12:14; 13:2–3). However, there is a darker side to this (v. 21), because what we say has a power of its own, and we can regret it as well as enjoy it. By speaking we can bring misfortune and misery, as well as joy, to ourselves and to others. Ahikar, the Assyrian sage of the seventh century BC, writes:

My son, sweeten thy tongue, and make savoury the opening of thy mouth,
   for the tail of a dog gives him bread, and his mouth gets him blows.

A good idea

Verse 22 begins, 'Find wife—find good', which suggests that it may be a popular proverb. Certainly the best kind of partner is meant—the author knows about the other kind (see 12:4). To make such a wise and happy choice is acceptable to God, and brings with it his 'favour', or goodwill.

Harsh realities

Verse 23 reports, without comment, something which happens all too often in all societies. In a social setting, those in comfortable circumstances have a natural advantage, while the less well-off are sometimes 'put in their place' or ignored altogether. The writer makes no comment, but leaves us to our own thoughts, which might well include a hard look at our personal and church relationships. Verse 24 contrasts the fair-weather friends, whose friendship is not really serious, with those who are constant through thick and thin. The two words for 'friend' are different; the second one describes a closer relationship, founded on love.

TO THINK ABOUT

Much of this passage is about relationships, good and bad. Jesus said, 'When you are offering your gift at the altar, if you remember that your brother or sister has something against you, leave your gift there before the altar and go; first be reconciled to your brother or sister, and then come and offer your gift.'
(Matthew 5:23–24)

PRAYER

Lord, may I be both wise and generous when I speak to or about others.

INTEGRITY & DECEIT

In verse 1, we might expect the opposite of 'poor' to be 'rich', and several versions of the Bible make the change, to match 28:6. However, the contrast here is between those who practise integrity even when they have every excuse to try deceitful ways, and the universal stupidity of crooked practice. It is not saying that the rich are automatically identified with fools or the poor with the upright, which would be against the general thought of Proverbs.

Verse 4 repeats what has already been said about poverty and wealth (see 18:23), and verse 6 enlarges on this, with its picture of the wealthy, generous, popular person. To 'seek the favour' of someone is literally 'to stroke their face'—that is, to soften them up!

The first two lines of verse 7 are harsh but realistic. The poor can become a burden and then a cause of resentment even to their families, and more so to friends who feel no obligation. 'Hate' is a strong word, especially in the Old Testament setting of family ties and duties, but it is all too possible when relatives add to financial problems.

The third line of the verse is difficult to understand. Literally it says, 'They who pursue word... they are not'; probably it is the remaining part of an incomplete couplet. The NRSV interprets it as describing the pitiful appeals for help and the disregard of so-called friends.

Following the 'better' of verse 1 is the 'not good' of verse 2. Heedless pursuit of our own wishes leads to hasty and unconsidered action, and we find ourselves disastrously following the wrong path. The result is likely to be that we get nowhere. Unwilling to admit our mistake, we put the blame on God.

Apart from being a shrewd observation on human nature, this argues against the idea that failure is God's work. The responsibility lies with us:

Do not say, 'The Lord is to blame for my failure';
  it is for you to avoid doing what he hates

                                       (Ecclesiasticus 15:11, NEB).

About perjury

The seriousness of this offence (vv. 5, 9) cannot be emphasized too strongly or too often (see, for example, 6:19; 14:5, 25). The only difference between these two verses is that the penalty is more severe in verse 9.

This is sometimes taken as evidence of the justice of the legal system of the time, but it might also be interpreted as describing the ideal, while the reality is that miscarriages of justice do occur in spite of the strictness of the law. The case of Jesus himself is one such example.

Knowing ourselves

Wisdom and understanding are parallel in verse 8, meaning proper perception and insight. To attain these, often we must first deal with a poor self-image. This does not mean that we become arrogant, but that we seek the self-knowledge which will rid of us of the lack of self-esteem which can cripple our progress in every sphere. The confidence described in this verse is strengthened for the Christian by the promise that 'you are a chosen race, a royal priesthood, a holy nation, God's own people, in order that you may proclaim the mighty acts of him who called you out of darkness into his marvellous light' (1 Peter 2:9).

PRAYER

Lord, give me contentment, generosity and the confidence which comes from trust in your unfailing love.

HOW UNSUITABLE!

Verse 10 describes two incongruous situations. First, there is an igno-rant and unappreciative person in the lap of luxury—as inappropri-ate as the fool's 'fine speech' in 17:7. Luxury has its value and uses, but if it is misused and misunderstood it develops our worst quali-ties. Second, there is a slave elevated to political power. A slave in command is not unknown in Proverbs, and can be a good thing (see 17:2), but there is always the danger of arrogance and tyranny.

It is quite usual to find in the literature of the time lists of such absurdities; for example:

> ...*a poor man who boasts,*
> *a rich man who lies,*
> *and an old fool who commits adultery* (Ecclesiasticus 25:2, NEB).

Wrath and mercy

To be 'slow to anger', or to 'defer our anger' (v. 11) (presumably until we have cooled down), is wise as well as right. 'Their glory' can also mean 'their beauty', which turns the rather quiet and everyday virtue of forbearance into something glowing and splendid. It is one of God's characteristics.

Verse 12 has a lesson both for the king's subjects (it is not wise to provoke a lion), and for the king himself (mercy is as quietly effective as dew). The king's displeasure is to be treated with respect: see also 16:14–15.

Home and family

The first part of verse 13 repeats the sad observation of 17:21. The second part, although it is drily humorous, still describes a situation which drives everybody to complete exasperation. There is an Arab proverb (quoted by Delitzsche in his commentary) which says:

> *Three things make a house intolerable:*
> *Tak (the rain leaking through),*
> *Nak (a wife's nagging), and*
> *Bak (bugs).*

Verse 14 makes two contrasts. The first is between the nagging wife of verse 13 and the partner who is half of a marriage which has God's blessing. The second is between the inheritance from our parents which is an accident of birth, and the God-given gift of a wife who has insight and discretion.

In the earlier Old Testament, a young man's wife is usually (Genesis 24:2–4), though not always (Judges 14:2), chosen by his parents. Later, there is more freedom (see 18:22), so a happy choice is seen as the outcome of divine guidance.

More about laziness

Laziness is not static, but has a life of its own. It creeps up on us imperceptibly, like going to sleep (v. 15), and the end result in an extreme case is virtual insensibility to what is going on around us— we might as well be unconscious. On a more practical note, like 6:6–11 and 12:24, this points out that if we do not work we shall starve.

Obedience gives life

Opinions are divided about verse 16. The 'commandment' may mean God's Law, written in the Scriptures, in which case 'their ways' must be taken as 'God's ways'. But as there is no mention of God, this may be about the guidance given by parents or teachers of wisdom, in which case we are being warned that unless we have a right rule of life we shall 'die'. This could mean anything from a gradual loss of any meaning in life to literal loss of life—not unreasonably, since Proverbs regards death as the natural consequence of wrongdoing. Whichever interpretation we accept, the principle is the same, but in the first case it is God who deals out reward or punishment, and in the second, we determine our own fate.

PRAYER

O Thou, who art the author of all good things in Thy holy Church… control us all, and so govern our thoughts and deeds, that we may serve Thee in righteousness and true holiness.

Philip Melanchthon (1497–1560)

KINDNESS REWARDED

The prophets strongly condemn any lack of proper justice for the poor; for example:

> Ah, you who make iniquitous decrees,
>> who write oppressive statutes,
> to turn aside the needy from justice
>> and to rob the poor of my people of their right... (Isaiah 10:1–2).

The Wisdom writers show the same concern, but here in verse 17 justice is not simply a matter of refraining from oppression. Active, generous measures must be taken to help the disadvantaged. When we give unstintingly, we are giving to God; when we do not give, it is him whom we insult (see 14:31; 17:5; Matthew 25:40, 45). Here, the promised recompense, typical of Proverbs, is prosperity in this life, though it is doubtful if this means literally getting our money back! The New Testament goes further and holds out the prospect of reward in heaven. Jesus says, 'Everyone who has left houses or brothers or sisters or father or mother or children or fields, for my name's sake, will receive a hundredfold, and will inherit eternal life' (Matthew 19:29).

Thinking about discipline

To neglect discipline while children are young and impressionable (v. 18) does them no favours, but can contribute to their eventual ruin (see also 13:24). Although, in accordance with the custom of the time, this verse is probably talking about corporal punishment, the second line is not to be taken as a warning against wishing for our off-springs' demise—this would be totally alien to the picture of family life painted by Proverbs. Rather, it is a warning about what we may do to them by weakness and over-indulgence.

Verse 19, although difficult to translate, is clearly making a point about disciplining ourselves. An uncontrollable temper will repeatedly land us in trouble, however often someone rescues us from its consequences.

Deferred satisfaction

In accordance with the spirit of our age, instant gratification is to be desired. However, here (v. 20), learning from the wise advice of others is seen as a long-term investment for the future.

And in that future, it is not our plans but God's that are finally carried out. The proverb 'Man proposes but God disposes' (see v. 21) is common to other ages and cultures. An Egyptian papyrus reads, 'If fate and fortune come, it is God who sends them.'

Loyalty and steadfastness

The two halves of verse 22 do not fit easily together, but 'loyalty' is the faithful love which God shows to us, and which we should show in any relationship of friendship. Integrity, the product of such loyalty, matters more than wealth or position.

In verse 23, certain security and safety (probably here in a spiritual rather than a material sense) come from the reverent obedience to God which is the foundation of the wisdom that Proverbs commends as the ideal in life (1:7).

PRAYER

Lord, the lessons about self-discipline, patience, loyalty and obedience to you that these verses teach are not easy to learn. Please help me to understand them, and give me the will to carry them out.

TOO LAZY *to* EAT

Lazy people are of course deplorable, but somehow there is often something comical about them, as here in verse 24 and in verse 15. The picture is of a meal, eaten oriental style, with hands plunged into the communal dish. However, one who is seriously lazy cannot even get through the process of eating—the effort of lifting hand to mouth is too great! It may be that there is a wider meaning to this saying, directed towards those who start an activity but lack the application to finish it.

The scoffer, the simple and the fool

We have met all these characters before. The scoffers (see 1:22; 9:7–8; 13:1; 15:12) are not lacking in intelligence, but detest reproof, and so are unable to make any progress towards becoming wise (14:6). The simple (1:4, 32; 9:16) are naïve and gullible, but not unteachable. They can learn from the sight of the scoffer's deserved punishment (v. 25). The fools (10:23) simply do not want to know, and brush aside anything to do with wisdom. So, like the scoffers, they will incur punishment (v. 29)—here perhaps from other people rather than directly from God.

Family cruelty

An extreme case is described in verse 26. It seems that the death penalty for striking or cursing a parent in Exodus 21:15, 17 is no longer carried out. So violence, and appropriation of the property in which a (presumably widowed) mother is still living, although disgraceful, are within the law. The 'shame and reproach' are the more heartbreaking because they are brought about by the parents' own children. We inflict this same cruelty and rejection on God when we turn away from him:

> *I reared children and brought them up,*
>   *but they have rebelled against me* (Isaiah 1:2).

Words, useful and useless

Verse 27 is the only time that 'my child' is addressed in this section of Proverbs (10:1—22:26). It may be that this verse originally belonged in chapters 1—9 and was moved here because it follows the dreadful example of the children described in verse 26. It is not easy to translate, but its purpose is to warn against the danger of departing from truth—a caution repeated more solemnly in 2 Peter 2:21: 'For it would have been better for them never to have known the way of righteousness than, after knowing it, to turn back from the holy commandment that was passed on to them.'

In verse 28 we are back in the law court. The 'worthless witness', or 'scoundrel' (see 6:12), has a wholly cynical attitude to the course of justice, while the wicked positively gulp down anything that is malicious or tainted, with every appearance of pleasure.

TO THINK ABOUT

There are several unpleasant characters in this passage: the lazy, the stubborn, the callous, the liar, the unpleasant gossip. Do we see anything of ourselves in any of these?

PRAYER

Search me, O God, and know my heart;
test me and know my thoughts.
See if there is any wicked way in me,
and lead me in the way everlasting.
(Psalm 139:23–24)

The DANGER *of* EXCESS

Wine and 'strong drink', or mead—probably the distilled juice of fruits other than grapes—is a common drink in the Bible, only forbidden to those who, like the Rechabites, have taken a vow to abstain (Jeremiah 35:5–6). However, here in verse 1 it takes on a life of its own and behaves like someone who has taken too much of it—a 'mocker' (the same word as 'scoffer' in 19:29), and a brawler, noisy and violent. 'Led astray' is literally 'lurches' or 'reels'—a suitable double meaning!

Royal anger and royal judgment

Verse 2 is a reminder (see 16:14) that kings are to be treated with respect and some caution—their anger is not only threatening (see 19:12) but can carry dread consequences for the tactless subject. However, verse 8, like 16:10, credits the king with sound judgment. It is possible for one in authority to have a practised eye, and to be able to sift the wheat from the chaff when confronted with a situation requiring judgment. 1 Corinthians 2:15 extends this gift beyond those in power to anyone who seeks it: 'Those who are spiritual discern all things, and they are themselves subject to no one else's scrutiny.'

Think before you speak

The person who is commended by the Wisdom writers is never the noisy, loud-mouthed, impetuous, quarrelsome attention seeker, but the one who 'refrains', or 'keeps aloof' from trouble (v. 3). This is not saying that we should remain silent when there is injustice, but it does mean resisting the temptation to pick a quarrel (see 17:14). Possibly it is a warning not to defend ourselves; our example in this very difficult act of self-control is Jesus: 'When he was abused, he did not return abuse; when he suffered, he did not threaten; but he entrusted himself to the one who judges justly' (1 Peter 2:23).

Cause and effect

The season for ploughing is immediately after the harvest, so that the next crop can be sown before the winter rains come. The lazybones

(v. 4), perhaps worn out by the effort of harvesting, perhaps disliking the colder weather, or more likely from general inertia, does not do the necessary work and consequently has nothing to reap. Some commentaries suggest that rather than accepting this natural justice, sluggards are actually surprised when the soft option does not produce results.

Fathoming one's fellows

Proverbs does not hold the view that everyone must have hidden depths of wisdom (see 14:12; 16:22), but it does encourage us to develop the gift of discernment, so that we can understand and draw out the plans of others, and perhaps help to put them into operation. Verse 5 is not about dreaming great thoughts, it is about the practical use of intelligence.

It is easy to make declarations of friendship and loyalty; the test comes when these good intentions need to be put into practice, and such absolute reliability is sadly rare (v. 6). There is no moral intended here; the writer simply states a fact of life with which most if not all of us will be able to identify.

Integrity and the family

In the Old Testament, divine blessing, as well as punishment, will be extended to one's descendants (Exodus 20:5–6). So the best legacy that children can receive is not wealth or status, but the example of a godly life (v. 7).

TO THINK ABOUT

Happy are those whose way is blameless,
who walk in the law of the Lord.
Happy are those who keep his decrees,
who seek him with their whole heart,
who also do not wrong,
but walk in his ways.
(Psalm 119:1–3)

A QUESTION *for* EVERYBODY

The answer to the question in verse 9 must be 'Nobody'. The sinfulness of the human heart is presupposed in the Old Testament, (although rather surprisingly the story in Genesis 3 is not used in evidence) and spelt out explicitly in some of its later writings. For example: 'Surely there is no one on earth so righteous as to do good without ever sinning' (Ecclesiastes 7:20).

We cannot even judge how sincere we are when we acknowledge and repent of our sins; only God can do that (16:2). According to Proverbs, the answer is to strive for righteousness and integrity; the Christian has the assurance that 'by grace you have been saved through faith, and this is not your own doing; it is the gift of God— not the result of works, so that no one may boast' (Ephesians 2:8–9).

A window on commerce

Verse 10 repeats the strong warning of 11:1 about the extreme unacceptability of giving short measure. Verse 14 is a vivid picture of oriental trading, of which haggling is a feature. The buyer complains loudly that the purchase is too expensive, and then boasts about an excellent bargain. There is no moral message here—this is how life is.

Early warning

In chapters 1—9, 'child' means a young adult; in chapters 10—21, it means one still living at home in the care of parents. Here in verse 11, the implication is that character is formed early, and does not change, and the unspoken advice is that early influences are important (see 22:6). But this verse need not apply only to the young. Throughout our lives, our behaviour reflects what we are; Jesus says, 'You will know them by their fruits' (Matthew 7:20).

Verse 12 can be understood in more than one way. It may be saying that the reliability of the product is guaranteed by the maker, or it may be a teacher's coded exhortation to pay attention—since eyes and ears are made by God, they need to be used properly. A third, though perhaps less likely, meaning is that because 'hearing' can also mean 'obedient' and 'understanding', we owe our first loyalty to God who made us.

The warning of 6:9–10 is again repeated in verse 13. Laziness is as easy and pleasant as falling asleep, but it does not make for prosperity. That must be earned by alert industry.

More precious than jewels

Verse 15 is not despising wealth (it would be against the whole teaching of Proverbs if it did!) but it observes that intelligent, knowledgeable words have a value exceeding even the most precious jewels (see 3:14–15; 8:10–11). 'Precious jewel' can mean either a personal ornament or a treasured piece of household furnishing. Ptah-hotep writes, 'Good speech is more hidden than the emerald.'

TO THINK ABOUT

Much of this is about what matters most—our standing before God as his creation, our character and conduct, our shortcomings, our priorities, and the way we live our lives. Do we take time to think and pray about it all, or are we too busy?

PRAYER

Lord, forgive me that so often I do not give you the time which I owe you. Help me to put you first.

66 PROVERBS 20:16–23

A DOUBTFUL CASE

The situation described in verse 16 is clear; the meaning is not so obvious. According to Exodus 22:25–26, it is permitted to take a person's cloak as security for a loan. So the message here may be that the same practice may legally be followed if you are dealing with someone who is standing surety for a third party. Or it may be a simple warning not to lend without security. However, the advice elsewhere in Proverbs (6:1–5; 11:15) is against acting as surety for anybody, in which case this is a sharp rebuke. If anyone has been foolish enough to be responsible for another's debt, more fool them! The guarantor's own garment must be confiscated. In view of the general attitude to giving guarantees, especially to 'strangers', or foreigners, the last interpretation seems the likeliest.

Ill-gotten gains

Verses 17, 21 and 23 all convey a feeling of sharp practice. In verse 17 this is explicit: wealth gained by fraudulent means may be enjoyable at the time, but, perhaps because it has cost little effort, it will later quite literally turn to dust and ashes. In verse 21, the inheritance gained 'quickly' (or 'prematurely'), perhaps without waiting for the appointed time, will not bring lasting happiness—the 'end' may even mean divine retribution (5:4). Verse 23 yet again warns against dishonesty in business—the practice of using false weights and measures is always singled out for particular condemnation (see v. 10). The more general message of these examples must be that wickedness does not pay in the long run.

Take advice and plan carefully

It is seldom, if ever, wise to 'go it alone' when planning some major project. The 'counsel' and 'guidance' must be sound—such as Wisdom herself would give (see 8:14)—and the implications of the whole thing must be thought through. Jesus asks, 'What king, going out to wage war against another king, will not sit down first and consider whether he is able with ten thousand to oppose the one who comes against him with twenty thousand?' (Luke 14:31).

The indiscreet gossip (v. 19), unable to keep a secret and therefore unable to keep yours, has already figured (10:14; 11:13). The 'babbler' may not be malicious, but is certainly stupid—the root of the word is the same as that of the 'simpleton'. Keep well clear of such people.

More serious is the sin of putting a curse on our parents (v. 20). In Exodus 21:17, the punishment for this offence is death; in later Judaism, this may have been modified to religious and social exclusion:

> *To leave your father in the lurch is like blasphemy,*
> *and to provoke your mother's anger is to call down the Lord's curse*
> > (Ecclesiasticus 3:16, NEB).

The message of the Old Testament is that parents are to be honoured and respected, and this is confirmed by the New: 'Children, obey your parents in the Lord, for this is right. "Honour your father and mother... so that it may be well with you and you may live long on the earth"' (Ephesians 6:1–3).

Beware of vengeance

The thought of revenge is very attractive (v. 22), especially if the opportunity is there; but here again, the principle of non-retaliation runs throughout the Bible. Paul, loosely quoting Deuteronomy 32:35, writes: 'Beloved, never avenge yourselves, but leave room for the wrath of God; for it is written, "Vengeance is mine, I will repay, says the Lord"' (Romans 12:19).

'Wait for the Lord and he will help (or save) you' may mean here that justice will take the form of rescue rather than punishment.

PRAYER

Lord, I find it hard to be forgiving, and I never want to lose the chance to pay somebody back. Please give me your Spirit, so that I can leave it to you to deal with those who have hurt me. And may I have something of your love and compassion for them.

HUMBLE DEPENDENCE
& RASH PROMISES

The sayings about guidance (16:1, 9; 19:21) all have a slightly different emphasis—God's answers, God's plans, God's purpose. Here (v. 24), we have to face the limitations of our own knowledge, and our need humbly to acknowledge God's insight and power which direct our lives.

This represents one strain of thought in Proverbs—the sovereignty of God. The other—human freedom and responsibility—is expressed in verse 25. To say, 'It is holy' means to dedicate something to God, and this is not to be taken back, so we must think carefully before we make such a promise. The principle is that of the Wisdom writers about avoiding hasty or unconsidered action, here applied to religious matters.

These two attitudes to life coexist side by side, and no attempt is made to reconcile them; they appear elsewhere in the Wisdom books—for example:

> *Do not yield to every impulse you can gratify*
> *or follow the desires of your heart.*
> *Do not say, 'I am my own master';*
> *you may be sure the Lord will call you to account*

(Ecclesiasticus 5:2–3, NEB).

More about the king

The king's authority and responsibilities are described in 16:10–15 and elsewhere (for example, 19:12). Verses 26 and 28 add to the picture. The king not only discerns what is evil (see also v. 8); he takes action against it (v. 26). The 'wheel' is the wheel of the threshing-cart which goes backwards and forwards to separate the wheat from the chaff. Its use represents severe punishment; in Amos 1:3 the Syrians are condemned because 'they have threshed Gilead with threshing sledges of iron'.

But with justice there is mercy. The combination of loyalty and faithfulness (see 3:3; 14:22; 16:6) always means the highest standard of moral excellence, since these are characteristics of God himself:

His steadfast love (loyalty) endures for ever,
and his faithfulness to all generations (Psalm 100:5).

Here (v. 28), loyalty and faithfulness are personified as protectors of the king's person, and righteousness (a free translation—the original repeats 'faithfulness') as the upholder of his throne. The king is responsible for preserving God's standards, and is in turn protected by them.

God's searching lamp

The 'lamp' (v. 27) is usually understood to be our God-given conscience—that in us which distinguishes us from the animals, and makes us able to examine our own natures and motives. The underlying thought is that this moral perception is not only part of God's creation, but is evidence that God himself is in us.

At our best

'Glory' here (v. 29) means 'adornment', and one of the attractions of youth is its physical strength. But every age has its own beauty, including old age—perhaps particularly old age since, as we have seen (16:31), in this society the old are not regarded as 'past it' but are highly respected. Long life means not only God's favour, but also the acquisition of the wisdom which comes with experience.

A sluggish conscience or wickedness in the depth of our being (v. 30) needs dealing with in a way that may not be pleasant but will undoubtedly be beneficial. The Old Testament is sometimes accused of being too given to advising corporal punishment (see 13:24), but the sense of this verse is that moral evil must be put down by severe measures; nothing half-hearted will do.

PRAYER

Lord, you know all about me and I cannot hide anything from you.
Please help me to face the things which only you and I see, and
show me how to begin to deal with them.

68   PROVERBS 21:1–7

GOD *is in* CONTROL

Verse 1 puts the king's power into perspective; like everyone else he is subject to God's overriding providence. His 'heart', or will, is like a 'stream of water' in God's hand. To manage a stream of water sounds an unlikely operation, but the comparison is probably with the irrigation system in countries like Egypt and Babylonia, controlled by artificial dams and canals.

What applies to the king applies to us all. Verse 2 repeats the thought of 16:2, and re-emphasizes the contrast between our imperfect perception—little more than guesswork—and God's certain knowledge and understanding of ourselves and our intentions, motivations and actions.

Ritual and sincerity

There is noting wrong with sacrifice in itself: it is commanded by the Law, and is meant as a sign of love and obedience towards God. However, it is less important than other things, such as the spirit in which it is offered, and the lifestyle of the offerer. Proverbs makes this point more than once (see 15:8), and is at one with the prophets (see Amos 5:22). Indeed, throughout the Wisdom writings runs the warning that we cannot buy God's favour:

> *The Most High is not pleased with the offering of the godless,*
> *nor do endless sacrifices win his forgiveness*
>
> (Ecclesiasticus 34:19, NEB).

A false guide

Verse 4 reads literally, '…the ploughing of the wicked (presumably their livelihood) is sin'; the NRSV has taken the translation of the Greek Old Testament, making a small alteration and substituting 'lamp' for 'ploughing'. Some commentators think that the verse consists of two unconnected parts, but as translated here it points out the sinfulness of allowing arrogance and pride to be our 'guiding light', or our motivating force.

Successful planning

There is a get-rich-quick theme in verses 5 and 6 (see also 20:21). Careful planning based on hard work (v. 5) is more likely to yield long-term results than hasty or impetuous schemes, which often end by being loss-making.

Worse still is dishonest practice (v. 6); any gain is short-lived, like drifting smoke, and ends in destruction. The thought is similar to that of 14:12, but here death is pictured as a living creature, snaring the foolish and wicked as a hunter snares his prey. The end of it all is self-inflicted punishment (v. 7). Violence actually turns on its perpetrators and destroys them; they have only themselves to blame.

TO THINK ABOUT

Contrast what happens when we allow God to control our lives and plans, with the outcome of greed, self-will and dishonesty. Are we prepared to yield control to him, or are we determined to have our own way, using our own methods?

PRAYER

O Lord, we beseech thee mercifully to receive the prayers of thy people who call upon thee: and grant that they may both perceive and know what things they ought to do, and also may have grace and power faithfully to fulfil the same; through Jesus Christ our Lord.

Collect for the First Sunday after Epiphany, *Book of Common Prayer*

CONDUCT & ATTITUDE

There are a number of loosely connected thoughts in these verses, none of them reflecting much credit on human nature. There is the contrast (v. 8) between the wicked (translated here and in the RSV as 'the guilty', and in the REB as 'the criminal'), who follows a devious path; and the pure, or innocent, whose conduct is straightforward and honest.

There is the sad observation (v. 10; see also 10:23) that sometimes we sin not only through weakness but because we actually want to do so and enjoy it, and that often it is those closest to us whom we treat the worst.

There is the seriousness of behaving callously to the poor (v. 13; reiterating 17:5, and putting the negative aspect of the exhortations in 14:21, 31). Those who ignore the cries of the needy will find in their turn that they are not listened to—whether by their fellows or by God. The ultimate comment on this verse is the parable of the rich man and Lazarus in Luke 16:19–31.

And there is the pleasure which the righteous feel when they do justice or see it done (v. 15), and the dismay which goodness arouses in the wicked.

With the exception of verse 13, no moral is pointed, but the facts speak for themselves.

Harmony before luxury

It was possible to sleep on the roof of an oriental house, and even to build a simple guest-room there, as was provided for Elisha (2 Kings 4:10), but to live in such a constricted space would be both cramped and lonely. However, any privation with peace is better than luxury with quarrelling and disagreements (v. 9).

Effective education

The 'simple'—naïve and gullible but not unteachable—learn best from the object lesson of seeing the ineducable 'scoffer' punished. The wise are able to learn by direct instruction (v. 11). A similar idea is expressed in 19:25.

Who is the Righteous One?

It is not clear whether this figure (v. 12) is a human being or God himself, since both can observe and draw conclusions from what they see. However, only God is able to take effective action against the wicked—a person is unlikely to be able to bring about the ruin of another. This name is used only here and in Job 34:17, when God asks:

> *Will you condemn one who is righteous and mighty…*
> *who shows no partiality to nobles,*
>   *nor regards the rich more than the poor,*
>   *for they are all the work of his hands?*

Gifts and bribes

Verse 14 also can be understood in two ways. Either 'gift' and 'bribe' mean the same, in which case this is a comment on the usefulness of such inducements. Or, if 'gift' is used in a good sense and 'bribe' in a bad, there is condemnation of the practice of giving bribes. Other verses in Proverbs reflect both points of view: 18:16 is neutral, 15:27 and 17:23 are hostile, while 17:8 simply remarks what a useful tool a bribe can be.

PRAYER

Lord, I thank you that you know all about human nature and
its weaknesses. Please show me what is right in the perplexing
situations which I meet every day.

70 PROVERBS 21:16–23

TWO WARNINGS

Verse 16 may be saying that folly leads to premature death—the teaching of Proverbs that those who reject wisdom die prematurely. Or it may mean that a fool is as good as dead, because lack of wisdom means lack of the advantages which make up life in any real sense.

Whichever interpretation we choose, 'rest' does not mean repose or relaxation, but 'coming to rest' in the sense of taking up residence—whether with the 'assembly of the dead' in Sheol, or with those whose lives are worthless.

In verse 17, the warning is against excess. Pleasure, like wealth, is not wrong in itself, but where it leads to gluttony it brings no joy, but rather, poverty—whether material on account of extravagance, or spiritual. Wine and oil are the usual accompaniments of a feast; oil is used for personal adornment—see Amos 6:6: '…who drink wine from bowls, and anoint themselves with the finest oils'.

A life for a life

Verse 18 is reminiscent of 11:8—an apparent contradiction of 'the righteous' suffering for 'the unrighteous' (1 Peter 3:18) as demonstrated in the death of Jesus. A ransom is paid to free someone from the penalty which they are required to pay, so on a superficial reading this verse implies that if judgment is inflicted on a community the wicked are punished as substitutes for the righteous. However, this would be a crude interpretation, and against the principle of individual responsibility which is taught in Proverbs. It is probably a poetic way of saying that the wicked are likely to suffer the evil fate which they have planned for the righteous.

Solitude not strife

Verse 19 echoes the thought of verse 9 and of 19:13. The 'desert land' is sparsely populated and inhospitable, but at least it is quiet. Better social isolation than domestic quarrels. The authors of Proverbs clearly have strong feelings on this subject, judging by the number of times it crops up!

Two kinds of treasure

In verse 20, the treasure is material, and the contrast is made between the provident thrift of the wise and the extravagant ways of the foolish.

In verse 21, the treasure is spiritual. 'Righteousness and mercy'— the 'loyalty' of 3:3—are investments which will bring (long) life and honour, the gifts of Wisdom herself (see 3:16).

The most powerful weapon

Although verse 22 is hardly to be taken literally, it is true that when a successful military operation takes place, the commander who plans the operation is ultimately responsible for its success. The message is that the power of wisdom is superior to physical force.

How to keep out of trouble

Verse 23 is not the only place where caution in what we say is strongly advised (see 13:3; 18:21). The kind of 'trouble' into which our unguarded speech can lead us is when our words are repeated. It is safest to assume that there is no such thing as a completely safe environment:

> *Do not curse the king, even in your thoughts,*
>   *or curse the rich, even in your bedroom;*
> *for a bird of the air may carry your voice,*
>   *or some winged creature tell the matter* (Ecclesiastes 10:20).

PRAYER

Teach me to live, that I may dread
The grave as little as my bed;
Teach me to die, that so I may
Rise glorious at the awful day.

Bishop Thomas Ken (1637–1711)

UNPLEASANT CHARACTERS

The scoffer (v. 24) is already well known to us—one who hates correction (9:7–8) and deliberately flouts the moral law (1:22); who is not lacking in intelligence but whose wrong attitude is a barrier to gaining any godly insight (14:6); and who will eventually receive from God the same contempt that has been shown to God (3:34). This is one of the two formal definitions in Proverbs (see 24:8 for the other); it traces the scoffer's deplorable character to its root of pride and arrogance.

Another acquaintance is the lazybones (v. 25), who is dominated by desire (literally 'who desires desire', or 'covets greedily') but will not lift a finger to find satisfaction, since that would involve hard work. In 19:24 the lazy person cannot even be bothered to eat; here, this indolence reaches its logical conclusion—it is a killer, since no one can survive without the necessities of life.

The covetous (v. 26), who include the lazy of verse 25, only care for their own wishes, but, by contrast, one of the characteristics of the righteous is generosity.

Fourth in this rogues' gallery is the so-called worshipper (v. 27) who offers sacrifice for the wrong reasons. It has already been made clear (15:8; 21:3) that although there is nothing wrong with religious observances, sacrifice is unacceptable to God if it is not accompanied by an upright life. Here, 'evil intent' may mean hypocrisy—sacrificing in order to impress others—but it may mean something even more serious. Sacrifices were intended to cover sins committed inadvertently, or fraud of certain kinds; they were not meant to offer easy forgiveness for murder and adultery and such like. So that may be what is condemned here—an offering to secure safety at little cost (what is sometimes called 'cheap grace')—a too-facile act of repentance of which anyone is capable.

The good listener

The false witness will be punished (19:5, 9)—here (v. 28), with the severest punishment. The 'good listener' seems a strange contrast; we might expect to read 'the honest witness'. But anyone who cares enough to listen to others wants to know and understand, and is not pursuing a personal agenda. So they must in turn be worth listening to, and their testimony will carry weight.

The 'bold face' presented by the wicked is often bravado (v. 29), covering deceit. It is no substitute for sound principles, to which good people have given thought in order to achieve stability and establish their reputation. It is frequently the less flamboyant character who is the more genuine.

'Wisdom', 'understanding' and 'counsel' (v. 30) are almost identical in meaning, except that 'counsel' includes the ability to give advice. However, our best efforts will achieve nothing if we are fighting against God. Similarly, however well equipped we are physically (v. 31)—the horse was an essential part of the Israelite armed forces—we shall fail if we try to fight instead of God. Only he can give us success.

TO THINK ABOUT

Some common faults and failings are described in this passage—arrogance, laziness, greed, insincerity. Look again at verses 24–27, and ask God to show you what needs forgiveness in your life.

PRAYER

Hide your face from my sins,
and blot out all my iniquities.
Create in me a clean heart, O God,
and put a new and right spirit within me.
(Psalm 51:9–10)

BETTER *than* RICHES

Verse 1 echoes the thought of 10:7: reputation, particularly in a society which does not have very developed ideas about life after death and so places great emphasis on this life, is of the greatest importance.

In *Pirke Aboth*, or *The Sayings of the Fathers*—a Jewish book of wise comments and advice—we find this rabbinical teaching:

> There are three crowns:
>> the crown of the Torah (the law),
>> the crown of the Priesthood, and
>> the crown of kingship.
> But the crown of a good name excels them all.

It is also important for the Christian: we are told to 'abstain from every form of evil' (1 Thessalonians 5:22).

Verses 2 and 7 continue the theme of reputation. First (v. 2), whatever our social status, we are all created by God (see also 20:12). Second (v. 7), although we are all equal in God's sight, we do not all enjoy equally comfortable circumstances. Debt could force a whole family into slavery (Nehemiah 5:5), or a creditor might sell a debtor (Amos 2:6). What is probably being said is that poverty and borrowing invariably bring a state of dependence.

In both these verses, we are presented with a fact of life and left to draw our own conclusions, although elsewhere (see 14:31) we are reminded of our duty to those less fortunate than ourselves.

The 'clever' (v. 3) are not the intellectual or the coldly calculating, but the prudent and observant—those who act with forethought. The 'simple' are the naïve and gullible, who lack good sense. Both appear in 1:4.

An unthinking approach to life and its hazards sooner or later brings disaster. 'The simple... suffer' means literally 'they are fined'. In this case there is probably no legal penalty involved, only the price they pay for blind optimism and unconsidered actions.

In verse 5, caution is again advised, but this time calamity awaits not the foolish but the deliberately perverse (see 2:15). The 'thorns', like the snares, are probably hedges which are put in the way of trespassers;

Moffat translates the verse as 'On crooked courses men step into snares.'

'Humility' and the 'fear of the Lord' (v. 4) go together elsewhere in Proverbs (see 15:33)—perhaps they represent the non-religious and the religious versions of the same virtue. 'Riches and honour and (long) life' represent the ultimate in happiness to the writer; this verse is a forerunner of the saying which is usually interpreted in a more spiritual way: 'Blessed are the meek, for they shall inherit the earth' (Matthew 5:5).

Verse 8 describes the opposite consequence—the harvest of disaster which those who sow injustice and oppression will reap. The second part of the verse is not easy to interpret. It says literally, 'The rod of his fury will fall'—whether on the persecuted or eventually on the persecutor is not clear. The general intention must be to give encouragement to the oppressed; all questions will be answered at harvest-time:

> *For they sow the wind,*
> *and they shall reap the whirlwind* (Hosea 8:7).

In neither of these verses is a time given when the good and the evil will bear the consequences of their actions; the implication is that this will be in God's time, not ours.

The early years

The Wisdom writers are totally confident that it is early teaching which remains with us all our lives—thus handing to parents both a heavy responsibility and a wonderful opportunity. 'In the right way' (v. 6) (literally 'in his/her way') implies respect for children's individual needs and different characters, but not necessarily for their self-will (see 14:12).

This is, of course, only one of the many verses about the family. The writers know what a loving home can and should be (see, for example, 4:1–4), but are of the opinion that firmness and even at times severity are essential if children are to be given the right start in life (5:7–12; 13:24; 19:18).

PRAYER

Lord, help me to plan wisely both for myself
and for those whom I love.

SHARING BRINGS BLESSING

Verse 9 balances the rather stark observations in verses 2 and 7. Things need not be left as they are: it is within our power to do something to help the poor, and in doing so we shall ourselves find happiness. The virtue of generosity was acknowledged throughout the ancient Near East as well as throughout the Bible: the Egyptian papyrus *Insinger* reads, 'He who gives food to the poor will receive the infinite mercy of God.'

To add to all their other unpleasant characteristics (see comment on 21:24), scoffers are trouble-makers (v. 10): it is their pleasure to stir up quarrels even to the extent of instigating a lawsuit (the literal meaning of 'strife'). Their abusive talk does damage in a community, and sometimes the only remedy is to expel such members: 'If the member refuses to listen... tell it to the church; and if the offender refuses to listen even to the church, let such a one be to you as a Gentile and a tax collector' (Matthew 18:17).

Grace, truth and falsehood

Verse 11 is not easy to translate, but it appears to be advocating the acceptability of a combination of integrity and charm—not always found in one person. The king's approval does not mean favouritism, but suggests a realistic evaluation by one in authority, based on character rather than a superficial impression.

Verse 12 also presents difficulty since the eyes of the Lord usually rest on or are directed towards something; only here are they described as guarding and protecting. However, again we can infer the general meaning, which is a contrast between truth and lies. God cares about correct knowledge, and will deal with the words of the 'faithless', or the treacherous, who are likely to speak untruths.

An excuse and a repeated warning

Verse 13 adds to the already unflattering picture of the lazybones by imagining him or her dreaming up the idea that a lion is outside—so of course it is not possible to go to work. Although laziness is condemned throughout, this manifestation of it cannot help being laughable.

Warnings against the 'loose woman', or adulteress, have up to now belonged to the first part of the book (see chapters 2, 5, 6 and 7). Here (v. 14) and in the next chapter (23:27), the reader is reminded that her 'smooth words' (2:16) spell deep trouble, and that to heed them is to invite God's anger.

A perennial educational question

Is a child basically innocent, waiting for parents and teachers to impart what is good or bad, or is there an inborn foolishness—something more definite than inexperience (v. 15)? This has been a subject for debate among educationists for as long as education has existed; the writer has no doubt about the answer, or about how to deal with it.

Getting, not giving

There are two ways of understanding verse 16. Either it is saying that it is easier to get money from the poor than to wheedle it out of the rich, or it is warning us that neither oppressing the poor nor courting the rich will do us any good.

TO THINK ABOUT

This is the end of the long central section—the 'Proverbs of Solomon'—which began at 10:1. At times it has seemed like a random selection of thoughts, set down almost at the writer's will. But the connecting thread has been the wish to find out, 'How can we live a life that is pleasing to God?' Sometimes it may have been difficult to spot the answers, but the question has been consistent.

PRAYER

Teach me Thy way, O Lord,
Teach me Thy way!
Thy gracious aid afford,
Teach me Thy way!
Help me to walk aright,
More by faith, less by sight;
Lead me with heavenly light:
Teach me Thy way!

B. Mansell Ramsey (1849–1923)

74 PROVERBS 22:17–21

The WORDS *of the* WISE

Proverbs 22:17—24:34 is not the work of a single author, but a collection of the sayings of 'the wise', who seem to have been in a class of their own, like priests and prophets, and given equal respect. Jeremiah 18:18 speaks of 'instruction... from the priest... counsel from the wise... the word from the prophet'.

The 'thirty sayings' (22:22—24:22) are in some ways rather like the 'thirty chapters' in the Egyptian *Teaching of Amen-em-opet* dating from about 1000BC, which end:

> See for yourself these thirty chapters:
>   they entertain, they educate;
>   they are the foremost of all books;
>   they instruct the ignorant.

We do not know who borrowed from whom, but a number of themes are common. There are warnings against exploiting the poor (22:22–23); against relying too much on wealth (23:4–5); against moving ancient boundary stones (22:28; 23:10); and instructions on etiquette—for example, how to behave when you sit down to dinner with someone of rank (23:1–2)—which are all found in Amen-em-opet's 'Instructions'. However, there are important differences. Although some of this material is similar to that of Amen-em-opet, it is by no means a carbon copy; the choice has been selective, and there is distinctive Israelite teaching included. Also, the underlying philosophy of these chapters is not Egyptian. The 'wise' have based their material on the 'fear of the Lord'—the God of Israel, who takes up the cause of the poor (22:23) and who champions the orphans (23:11).

Back to school

Verses 17 and 18 bring us back to the educational atmosphere of chapters 1—9. It seems that they are in the first place addressed to the young who are in positions of some influence, but like all Wisdom teaching, they apply to people of every age. The tone is one of instruction rather than advice: 'Incline your ear... hear my words... apply your mind' (v. 17). The teacher calls the students to attention and reminds them of the benefits of doing so (v. 18): the more we learn, the more we can cope with life and so enjoy it.

What are we to learn?

The purpose of the 'thirty sayings' is 'to show you what is right and true, so that you may give a true answer to those who sent you' (v. 21). This was probably written to aspiring Court officials, entrusted with taking messages and relaying accurate answers. But the lesson is one for all times and situations, and is about more than accuracy. Ability to discharge such a duty reliably is a test of character and discretion. A useful prayer is:

Set a guard over my mouth, O Lord;
keep watch over the door of my lips (Psalm 141:3).

How do we learn?

These developing skills of perception, discretion, reliability and integrity are in proportion to a developing trust in God: 'So that your trust may be in the Lord, I have made them known to you today—yes, to you' (v. 19).

The personal note adds a feeling of urgency; from the beginning we must accept that we can only learn to represent the One whom we serve if we trust in him for our wisdom.

TO THINK ABOUT

This kind of learning is not an option. If we are to live in a way
which pleases God, we must submit to its discipline. Are we ever
guilty of thinking that we 'know it all'?

If any of you is lacking in wisdom, ask God, who gives to all
generously and ungrudgingly, and it will be given you.
(James 1:5)

CARE *for* OTHERS

The two sayings in verses 22–23 and 28 are a reminder about our attitude to the poor and needy in society. The poor must not be exploited, and the 'afflicted' (meaning 'the poor', but with an added emphasis on weakness and helplessness) are to be treated properly at 'the gate'—that is, the gate of the city where justice is administered (v. 22).

'Rob' and 'crush' are strong words; they underline the seriousness of an offence (perhaps even the offence of ignoring them) against the disadvantaged and the rejects of society, for God has a special concern for them (see Deuteronomy 24:14–15). When God pleads someone's cause, a special judgment is reserved for those who mistreat them (v. 23; see also Micah 7:9).

Another hazard of poverty at that time was the unscrupulous removal of land boundaries (v. 28), which is explained more fully in 23:10–11. Every household needed a 'landmark' to ensure its security, and there were certain property rights which must not be tampered with, particularly where land had come down by family inheritance (see Deuteronomy 19:14). However, it was fairly easy for the rich to override this law, and such disobedience did not go unpunished (Isaiah 5:8–10).

Verses 24 and 25 deal with our relationships with our peers. Uncontrolled anger can do a great deal of harm (v. 24), and it is wise to avoid friendship with someone whose ill-temper and hasty words are a way of life. Such a close association may end in our adopting just such a destructive attitude (v. 25)—destructive to ourselves as well as to others.

Foolish pledges

This is a common problem, and we have met it before in Proverbs (6:1–5; 11:15). To underwrite someone's debt will put your own possessions at risk if the debtor cannot pay. 'Why,' ask the wise men, 'get yourself into such a difficulty?' (vv. 26–27). Jesus, perhaps not only speaking of the cost of discipleship but with a situation such as this in mind, warns against embarking on any project without counting the cost:

For which of you, intending to build a tower, does not first sit down and estimate the cost, to see whether he has enough to complete it? Otherwise, when he has laid a foundation and is not able to finish, all who see it will begin to ridicule him, saying, 'This fellow began to build and was not able to finish' (Luke 14:28–30).

Always think things through, and avoid rash promises.

Good workmanship

Verse 29 is not so much an instruction as a brief comment on good craftsmanship and its rewards, in the context of the time, which regarded royal service as prestigious and fulfilling ('common people' means literally 'obscure'). If we are to live a godly life for others to see, we need to do our daily work as well and conscientiously as we can.

PRANYER

Almighty God,
whose Son, our Lord and Saviour Jesus Christ
was moved with compassion for all who had gone astray
and with indignation for all who had suffered wrong:
inflame our hearts with the burning fire of your love,
that we may seek out the lost,
have mercy on the fallen
and stand fast for truth and righteousness;
through Jesus Christ our Lord.

Pentecost 2, *Celebrating Common Prayer*

AMONG *the* RICH

When eating with someone of exalted rank, or any rank for that matter, there is appropriate and inappropriate behaviour. Here are three basic rules.

First, eat what is set before you (v. 1). Ptah-hotep writes, 'If you are among the guests of a man of higher rank, take what he offers when it is presented to you.' An alternative translation is 'observe whom is set before you', which would mean, 'Behave suitably in the presence of your host, thus showing consideration.'

Second, be careful not to let your appetite get the better of your manners (v. 2). 'Put a knife to your throat if you have a big appetite' is a vivid way of saying be restrained in your eating, and avoid gluttony.

Third, remember that another reason for not being greedy is that there may be some sinister motive behind the invitation—perhaps you are sitting down to 'the bread of deceit' (v. 3). Or it may simply be that your table manners are being observed and will be taken into account when the question of promotion arises.

Verses 4 and 5 are not decrying riches—that would be against the whole thinking of Proverbs. But although wealth is desirable, and is seen as the reward of uprightness and integrity, it is both wrong and useless to make its acquisition our be-all and end-all, for it is just as elusive as social position. There can be no guarantee that it will last (v. 5), and we certainly cannot take it with us when we die. Jesus tells the story of the man who set great store by his possessions, and ends: 'But God said to him, "You fool! This very night your life is being demanded of you. And the things you have prepared, whose will they be?"' (Luke 12:20).

Living as we do in a society whose obsession with the rich and famous is reflected in as well as fed by the media, this saying gives a salutary warning.

Eating with a grudging host

'Stingy' means literally 'one with an evil eye'—that is, one who is ill-natured, inhospitable and mean (v. 6).

The meaning of the first part of verse 7 is obscure; it can be, as here, 'a blocking of the throat', or, as in the RSV, 'For he is like one who is inwardly reckoning'—that is, watching every crumb that you eat. Either way, the result is the same—the behaviour of such a host literally makes us sick (v. 8)! These sayings are about behaviour to one's host, a matter of courtesy; moderation in the pursuit of material things, a matter of priorities; and discrimination in the choice of friends, a matter of common sense. But the theme which binds them together is that of greed—greed for food, for money, for companionship of any kind.

TO THINK ABOUT

What are the motives behind our decisions and behaviour? Do we remember Paul's exhortation to 'let love be genuine; hate what is evil, hold fast to what is good; love one another with mutual affection; outdo one another in showing honour'?
(Romans 12:9–10)

PRAYER

Lord, help me always to put you first, and correct me when I seek my own interests before yours or those of other people.

SAVE YOUR BREATH

'Do not speak in the hearing of' (v. 9) means literally 'Do not speak in the ears of'—indicating something said directly rather than something overheard. Since fools have no interest in the search for wisdom, and cannot imagine themselves to be mistaken, there comes a moment when it is a waste of time to try to give wise advice, whether it is about the fear of the Lord or simply everyday common sense. It is difficult to know when to stop, but it may help to remember the instruction which Jesus gave to his disciples: 'If any place will not welcome you and they refuse to hear you, as you leave, shake off the dust that is on your feet as a testimony against them' (Mark 6:11).

Protector of the poor

This is the second time within a few verses (see 22:28) that the prohibition against removing a land boundary is stressed (v. 10). It is particularly important to respect this law in the case of 'orphans' —which automatically means the underprivileged—since the landmark is their only protection against encroachment.

The 'redeemer' (v. 11) is the kinsman whose duty it is to intervene to prevent property from being sold outside the family. The Law is quite specific about it: 'If anyone of your kin falls into difficulty and sells a piece of property, then the next of kin shall come and redeem what the relative has sold' (Leviticus 25:25).

Here, as in Job 19:25, God himself 'redeems' or 'pleads the cause of' (a legal phrase meaning vindicating and avenging) those who have no human protector.

Wisdom's strict school

Commentators differ about exactly where the lines of demarcation between some of the sayings should come. Some think that verse 12 is a 'saying' on its own; others that it is simply a variation of 22:17. The most likely solution is probably to regard it as an introduction to these verses which remind us of the rigour, as well as of the joy, of seeking wisdom. 'Instruction' is the same word as 'discipline' in verse 13; willingness to learn, serious application to the task in hand and the acceptance of correction are essential if one is to be counted among 'the wise'.

Verse 13 is similar to a saying by Ahikar, the Assyrian writer from the seventh century BC (see 6:16–19):

Do not spare your son the rod,
or you will be unable to save him from wickedness.
If I strike you, my son, you will not die—
but if I leave you to your own devices you will not live.

This both endorses the fact that corporal punishment was accepted throughout the ancient world (see also 13:24), and stresses the benefits of correction. Whether verse 14 refers to escape from physical death (which seems likely), or from whatever retribution will fall on an undisciplined person in this life, it is saying that children will survive discipline—either in spite of it, or more probably because of it.

TO THINK ABOUT

Now, discipline always seems painful rather than pleasant
at the time, but later it yields the peaceful fruit of righteousness
to those who have been trained by it.
(Hebrews 12:11)

PRAYER

Lord, I do want to follow you, but I am not always sure what is
your will. Please help me to hear what you are saying to me when I
ask for guidance, and then to obey you.

A PERSONAL APPEAL

From here to 24:22, there is a change of style. In three places (23:15, 19; 24:13) the teaching is addressed to 'my child', taking us back to the more intimate atmosphere of the first nine chapters; verse 22 has 'Listen to your father.' The 'words of the wise' in this section come from the heart, and there is personal involvement with the pupils. In verse 16, 'soul' means literally 'kidneys', following the biblical custom of naming internal organs to express depth of feeling—rather as we say 'in my heart of hearts' or 'I feel it in my bones'. The point is being made that it is not only parents who have responsibilities: the young must make choices in how they behave and in what they say (v. 16).

True and false values

Envy (v. 17) comes from combined admiration and resentment, and it is particularly hard to fight when its objects are those who seem to prosper without any reference to God. Psalms 37 and 73 have a lot to say on this subject. For example:

> For I was envious of the arrogant;
>   I saw the prosperity of the wicked.
> For they have no pain;
>   their bodies are sound and sleek.
> They are not in trouble as others are;
>   they are not plagued like other people. (Psalm 73:3–5)

Part of the remedy lies in realizing that feelings of this kind come from an excessive preoccupation with the here and now, and with our own interests. The other two antidotes prescribed are perseverance (v. 17) in the fear of the Lord—the basic principle of Proverbs—and hope (v. 18). 'Future' carries with it the idea of an end—whether good (19:20) or bad (5:4). Here it is used in the positive sense: the promised 'end' for the righteous will be long life and prosperity (repeated in 24:14).

Choosing friends with discrimination

'The way' without any further description (v. 19) is used only here in Proverbs, perhaps unconsciously foreshadowing the early Church's name for Christianity: Paul says, 'I persecuted this Way up to the point of death' (Acts 22:4).

To walk in the right way calls for a decision, and that decision includes choosing the company we keep, and avoiding undesirable associates.

At first sight, we wonder whether there is anything more to say about gluttony and drunkenness, and the adverse effects of choosing our friends from among those who eat and drink to excess. However, verse 21 points out that greed and extravagance invariably lead to poverty, and that one of the ways in which this comes about is when the drowsiness which they induce affects the ability to do a day's work. 'The wise' have a clear work ethic, and would not be impressed with lengthy lunch breaks or extravagant expense claims!

TO THINK ABOUT

Although the tone of this passage is loving, it exposes some wrong feelings and false values. It also suggests some ways in which we can avoid or remedy these attitudes, which are as common now as they were then.

PRAYER

Lord, help me to resist following the crowd;
give me your perspective on life.

From ONE GENERATION *to* ANOTHER

Verse 22 is in line with the fifth Commandment (Exodus 20:12). When parents get old, relationships change, and the first consideration for their children is no longer obedience but loving duty and continuing respect. In Israel, as in the rest of the ancient Near East, reverence for parents was a 'must', although the problems were at least recognized:

> *My son, look after your father in his old age;*
>   *do nothing to vex him as long as he lives.*
> *Even if his mind fails, make allowances for him,*
>   *and do not despise him because you are in your prime.*
>   (Ecclesiasticus 3:12–13, NEB)

Proverbs has already warned us against heartlessness (19:26) and contempt (15:20) for the older generation; here, the positive aspect of the relationship is stressed.

However, love and appreciation are not to be one-sided. Just as the time for obedience has gone for the children, the time for applying discipline has passed for the parents. Now, there should be pride and appreciation (v. 24)—the result of the years of careful training (10:1; 13:1)—specially important in a society where the family is seen as living on in the children. So every generation takes pleasure in the others (v. 25; see also 17:6). These verses reinforce the pivotal role of the family, which is one of the themes running through Proverbs.

Valuable commodities

Verse 23 can be taken as a separate saying. Truth, wisdom, instruction or discipline, and understanding or insight (see 1:2) are not acquired without cost to ourselves in hard work and perseverance, but they are worth the effort of buying them. Once we have them, they are too precious to part with at any price.

A serious warning

Once again, the first words of verse 26 remind us of chapters 1—9; the importance of what is to come is emphasized by the words, 'Give me your heart', that is, 'Give me your full, undivided attention'. The wise teacher ventures to set himself up as a role model, inviting the pupil to observe and imitate (literally 'delight in') his way of life.

The prostitute and the adulteress (the 'alien woman' of 5:3) may represent two types of unchaste women, unmarried and married, both with the same destructive character (v. 27). Like the seductress of 7:12, they lie in wait for their victims, and yielding to their charms is like falling into a narrow, smooth-sided pit or well—it is extremely difficult to escape. However, this is not only about passively falling into the woman's clutches; she herself is on the attack, lying in wait like a brigand (v. 28), as 7:10–20 so vividly describes. The result of her activities is an increase in the 'faithless'—faithless to God's law (11:3, 6; 22:12), and untrustworthy in themselves (25:19). The implied advice is to keep well clear of such women.

TO THINK ABOUT

It is easy to take these instructions as belonging to another age, when the extended family was taken for granted, and adultery and prostitution were totally unacceptable in society. It is tempting to say 'times have changed', but have right and wrong changed? How should we conduct our family lives and educate our young people?

PRAYER

Lord, give us right judgment in all our decisions and attitudes.

The DRUNKARD—*in the* EYES *of* OTHERS

Verses 29–32 are different from the short, pithy sayings which are the most usual form of Wisdom teaching. They have something in common with the description of the adulteress in 7:6–23 in their vividness and their acute observation and insight.

They begin with a series of questions (v. 29), perhaps influenced by the use of 'riddles' as a teaching device (see 1:6), but more probably intended to emphasize the effect of chronic drunkenness—what we now call alcoholism—in the most telling way possible.

'Who has woe? Who has sorrow?' is literally 'Who has "Oh" and who has "Alas"?'—a series of painful exclamations. 'Who has strife?' refers to the ugly scuffles that people get into when they are drunk. 'Who has complaining?' means the magnifying of the trivial into a 'big deal'. 'Who has wounds without cause ?'—following on from the quarrels, the injuries that result from those slight and trivial differences. 'Who has redness of eyes?' probably speaks of the outward sign of dissipation, warning that people are not fit to work.

The answer (v. 30) is 'those who drink habitually and to excess', who 'linger late' and 'keep trying' different vintages; the 'mixed wine' may be wine blended with spices.

The wine of Canaan seems to have been red (v. 31): Genesis 49:11 refers to 'the blood of grapes'. The drunkard enjoys it when it 'sparkles in the cup'—that is, when the process of fermentation is complete and it 'goes straight down', or 'goes down smoothly':

> ...*like the best wine*
> *that goes down smoothly,*
> *gliding over lips and teeth* (Song of Solomon 7:9).

This descriptive passage ends with a warning. The effects of excessive drinking are not only deadly but insidious—like the silent, treacherous bite of a lethal snake (v. 32).

The drunkard—in their own eyes

Hallucinations, the inability to speak rationally, the sensation of being at the mercy of a universe that is out of control, and the loss of any sense of responsibility make up this dismal picture in verses 33–35.

The 'strange things' (v. 33) which the victims find themselves thinking and saying without their own volition are the 'perverse' words of 2:12 which twist right values and turn them upside down in irrational talk. Drunkards lose the ability to distinguish between right and wrong. 'Lying down in the midst of the sea' (v. 34) does not mean lying in the depths of the sea or on its surface, but describes the sensation of being on the high seas in a storm, when there is nothing stable beneath our feet and we cannot stand up. The word translated 'mast' occurs only here in the Old Testament and its meaning is uncertain; the REB has 'like one who clings to the top of the rigging', which probably conveys the essence of what is meant.

The first part of verse 35 may represent sheer bravado, or it may refer to loss of physical feeling—literally 'feeling no pain'. The last part is perhaps the saddest of all. The person who is truly addicted to alcohol learns nothing from experience, but only seeks more drink.

TO THINK ABOUT

This lively yet tragic picture confirms other teaching in Proverbs, for example 20:1 and 31:4–5, yet on the other hand, the authors also believe that wine can on occasion be a comfort to the dying and desperately distressed (31:5–6).

Perhaps the lesson is that we should exercise moderation in this and in all aspects of our lives.

PRAYER

Lord, thank you that your Son was the friend of the outcasts of society. Help us to follow his example, and to have compassion on those who are addicted to alcohol, whether we meet them at home or see them in our parks and shopping precincts. We ask for wisdom, endurance and love for their families, and for your guidance and strength for all who work among them.

81 PROVERBS 24:1–7

NOTHING *to* ENVY

Verses 1 and 2 underline the warning about undesirable friendships given in 23:19–21, and extends it from drunkards to all who are 'men of wickedness'—that is, who plot and carry out violence. Do not envy (literally 'be stirred up by') them, and do not imitate them. Instead, look at them closely. Everything about them is negative, and, contrary to appearances, real power does not rest with them, but with the wise (vv. 5–6).

Verses 3 and 4 can be interpreted in two ways. They may refer to the material rewards of following wisdom, understanding (or discernment) and knowledge, painting a picture of domestic stability and prosperity. This is in keeping with the general teaching of Proverbs—there is a practical incentive to follow God's ways, especially attractive in a society which is still learning to walk by faith. On the other hand, they may be symbolic: the beautiful, well-appointed house may mean the ordered and wholesome attitude to life that comes from sound values and a godly character.

Or again, they could refer back to chapter 9, where Wisdom is a woman who builds a house and gives an open invitation to all to share in the feast she has prepared, which will teach maturity and insight and point the way to a life that is worthwhile.

Whether this is about wisdom or Wisdom, the message is that it, or she, holds the key to material, moral and spiritual success.

Verses 5 and 6 resume the argument of verses 1 and 2, and adds to the desirability of wisdom. In any situation of conflict, it is not sheer physical strength but wise dealing and the willingness to accept good advice that bring victory (see 11:14; 20:18; 21:22).

Out of their depth

Fools cannot and will not seek wisdom (v. 7); they are by their own choice virtually ineducable—that is made clear throughout Proverbs. The second half of the verse is not so easy to understand, since one of the marks of a fool is a willingness to give an opinion on anything and everything without modesty or restraint (and with a great deal of noisy self-assertion—see 12:16; 18:6–7). However, there are occasions when the fool keeps quiet and, in so doing, can pass for a wise or intelligent person (17:28). 'The gate' is the place of administration and justice; the fool has no place there and may even know it. It is the voice of Wisdom which urgently needs to be heard.

TO THINK ABOUT

In the middle of much that is wrong in public life, Wisdom reappears. Her importance in public affairs cannot be overestimated—a reverent obedience to God's ways and commands can only be a good influence. The need for integrity and wise judgment among those in positions of authority is as great today as it was when Proverbs was written. It is still true that 'happy are the people to whom such blessings fall; happy are the people whose God is the Lord' (Psalm 144:15).

PRAYER

Lord, give your wisdom to all who have responsibilities in public affairs, and show me if there is any part, however small, that I should play.

FORFEITING PUBLIC RESPECT

Verses 8 and 9 are about scheming, and the scheming is calculated and malicious. The words for 'mischief-maker' (v. 8) and 'devising' come from the same root, which means something evil both in Proverbs and elsewhere. Leviticus 18:17 has 'it is depravity'; Judges 20:6, 'vile outrage'. To make matters worse, the 'scoffer' (see 1:22; 9:8; 13:1; 14:6; 21:11, 24) is associated with this piece of wickedness, so it is heartless as well as deliberate and brazen. Proverbs is full of things which are an 'abomination' to God—among them crooked ways (3:32), the list of sins in 6:16–19, false weights (11:1), and insincere worship (15:8). Here, the activities of the scoffer are utterly repugnant to all ordinary, decent people (v. 9).

Two tests of calibre

The NRSV makes the failures and sins of these verses all subject to the judgment at the end of verse 12. Other versions—RSV, REB and NIV—make verse 10 a separate saying. But the meaning is the same in either case. Weakness in the face of disaster (v. 10), failure to take courageous action (v. 11), and using ignorance as an excuse (v. 12), are not acceptable. However we try to cover up these deficiencies, God, who sees everything, is not deceived. The lack of social responsibility in verse 11 may refer literally to standing by while unjustly condemned prisoners are dragged off to execution, but it is unlikely that the bystander can do anything about that. It seems more likely to be about passers-by who, then as now, turn a blind eye to violence because they do not wish to be involved, and then try to deny all knowledge of the affair. The idea of actions being weighed and punishment administered is common to the Wisdom writers not only in Israel (see 16:2; 21:2) but also in Egypt, where the god Thoth was said to 'weigh the hearts of men'.

Wisdom and honey

Anything which is compared to honey is desirable (16:24), and not only in Proverbs:

The ordinances of the Lord are true
  and righteous altogether.
More to be desired are they than gold,
  even much fine gold;
sweeter also than honey,
  and drippings of the honeycomb (**Psalm** 19:9–10).

So in spite of its stringent demands, wisdom is good not only now but as an investment for the time to come (v. 14; see 23:17–18). It is worth finding and keeping; unlike eating honey, it is not a mere passing pleasure—it gives both present satisfaction and future hope.

TO THINK ABOUT

Verses 8–12 paint a dismal picture of how we can lose our self-respect, the esteem of others, and the approval of God. The way to avoid these errors is in verses 13 and 14; the way of wisdom is satisfying and fortifying as well as challenging.

PRAYER

Lord, give me the desire for the wisdom that comes from you, and give me the resolve to resist the evil thoughts, words and actions which displease you.

83 PROVERBS 24:15-22

BEWARE *of* VIOLENCE

To attack the home (literally 'pasture', or 'lair') of the righteous (v. 15), either secretly or openly, is self-defeating. The disaster they have inflicted will in turn fall on the perpetrators (v. 16). The righteous are resilient and will rise above misfortune ('seven times' means an indefinite number), but the wicked have no such resource, and once they are down they do not recover.. This appeal to self-interest is probably the only one which will reach the sort of person who is contemplating actions like these, and is a salutary reminder that an unscrupulous victory is seldom, if ever, lasting.

Beware of gloating

To 'rejoice' (v. 17) can mean a generous expression of pleasure (see 5:18; 23:25), or it can be malicious when it is at someone else's expense. Those who gloat over their enemies' misfortune may be more culpable than the enemies themselves, and God's judgment will be diverted to them (vv. 17–18).

It is harder still to feel positive sympathy with our opponents, and to remember that God loves them as he loves us. This is not expressed here, but is probably implied. Jesus said, 'Love your enemies and pray for those who persecute you, so that you may be children of your Father in heaven; for he makes his sun rise on the evil and the good, and sends rain on the righteous and on the unrighteous' (Matthew 5:44–45).

Beware of fretfulness

'Do not fret' (v. 19) means 'do not get over-excited'. There is a hopeful future for the godly (23:18), but no future at all for the wicked (v. 20)—evil cannot expect a good outcome (13:9). The psalmist gives the same advice:

> *Do not fret because of the wicked;*
> *do not be envious of wrongdoers,*
> *for they will soon fade like the grass,*
> *and wither like the green herb* (Psalm 37:1–2).

The good citizen

The last of the 'thirty sayings' is positive, after several negative instructions. The text is not easy, because 'do not disobey either of them'—that is, God and the king (v. 21)—can also be translated 'do not associate with those who change', which may refer to the unpredictability of human authority, especially in a society where so much depended on the whim of the current ruler. However, the general message seems clear. Part of godliness is good citizenship, and this is also taught in the New Testament. For example, 'Honour everyone. Love the family of believers. Fear God. Honour the emperor' (1 Peter 2:17).

TO THINK ABOUT

It is fairly easy to agree with these reminders to avoid certain attitudes—though not always easy to carry them out. However, the question of submission to authority is more difficult. When we feel strongly that the law is wrong, should we still keep it? And how are we to register our disagreement? Jesus was prepared to pay taxes (Matthew 17:27) but was equally clear that God's requirements should be fulfilled (Mark 12:17). How can we know what is right, and how best can we make our point?

PRAYER

Thank you, Lord, for all the teaching in these 'thirty sayings', and for the help it gives in so many situations. May I remember and act on it when I have to make decisions, and give me your wisdom at all times.

More 'Words *of the* Wise'

It seems from the heading that these last verses of chapter 24 are a kind of appendix to 22:17—24:22 (in the Greek Old Testament they are placed at the very end of the book). They fit well here, because they are in the same style as what has gone before—some longer sections, some short two-line sayings.

Behaviour in the law courts

Probably addressed to judges and future judges, verse 23 echoes 18:5. It assumes that all civilized countries have a code of conduct governing their law (v. 24), and to violate this by showing partiality and unjustified lenience towards the 'wicked'—or, more probably, the 'guilty'—is unacceptable.

Verse 25 can be read as a continuation of verse 24: it is wrong to declare the guilty innocent, and correspondingly right to condemn them. However, 'rebuke' is not used elsewhere in Proverbs in a legal sense, so this may be about generally reproving wrongdoers rather than a reference to behaviour in court. If so, it connects with verse 26, where plain speaking is commended. The 'kiss on the lips' is an expression meaning friendship; a true friend will give an honest opinion, whether or not it is what the other person wants to hear.

Against groundless accusations

Verse 28 is not about futile private quarrels, as in 3:30, but about lying in court. It is yet another thing which is an abomination to God (see 24:9), and it is expressly forbidden in the Law: 'The judges shall make a thorough inquiry. If the witness is a false witness, having testified falsely against another, then you shall do to the false witness just as the false witness had meant to do to the other' (Deuteronomy 19:18–19).

Vengeance is also strongly condemned (v. 29; see 20:22), and not only in Israel. Amen-em-opet writes:

> *Unto him that doeth thee evil shalt thou return good.*
>   *Unto thine enemy, justice shalt thou mete out.*

The New Testament goes further in the Sermon on the Mount:

You have heard that it was said, 'You shall love your neighbour and hate your enemy.' But I say to you, Love your enemies, and pray for those who persecute you... For if you love those who love you, what reward do you have? Do not even the tax collectors do the same?

(Matthew 5:43–44, 46)

First things first

Verse 27 can be read in two ways. On the practical level, it reminds the farmer to have the right priorities. Make sure the land is in good order, producing enough to live on, before you settle down in comfort in the farmhouse. However, 'building a house' can also mean bringing up a family (see 14:1), so at another level we are reminded that a well-ordered life should be established before we take on other responsibilities. The message is, 'Sort out your life before you make serious commitments.'

This supplement (vv. 23–29) to the 'thirty sayings' of 22:17—24:22 includes a number of verses beginning, 'Do not', warning against injustice, perjury, vengefulness and laziness. However, it is not all negative: we are encouraged to be honest with our friends (v. 26), and to be prudent and sensible in planning ahead (v. 27). The way of godly wisdom is not simply a series of prohibitions; it means vigorously putting into practice the things which are right and sensible.

PRAYER

Lord, a lot of this is about truth. Help me not only to speak the truth, but to speak it with kindness as well as honesty. And show me when I am deceiving myself as well as others. Remind me, too, always to remember in my prayers those who live in countries where justice as we know it, under the official legal system, does not exist.

A STORY of NEGLECT

These verses are different from those which we have just read; they use the teaching device of narrative—which we have already met in the stories of the godly home (4:1–4), the adulteress and the naïve young man (7:6–23), and the drunkard (23:29–35)—to make a point. The point, that dire poverty arrives without warning on the heels of idleness, is identical with that made in 6:10–11, but it is reached by a different route. In chapter 6, the ant is held up as an example of industry and prudence, in contrast to the lazybones who needs to be prodded into activity and to learn that there are times in the year when extra effort is called for. Here, there is no call for action, but a certain hopelessness in the sad picture of what can happen if laziness is unchecked. Different teachers use different methods.

The owner of the vineyard is in no way a freak. This is an ordinary person who has made excuses, refused to look reality in the face, and postponed necessary action for too long, and the reason is not a lack of physical strength but of intelligence—literally 'empty-mindedness' (v. 30). There has been no attempt at prudence or planning, much less hard work.

The result is the vineyard which is not only unproductive and unprotected, but producing the wrong things (v. 31). 'Thorns' and 'thistles' are unusual Hebrew words: 'thorns' appears only here in the Old Testament; 'thistles' (or 'nettles') appears here, as well as in Zephaniah 2:9, describing the future devastation of the land of Moab, and Job 30:7, where it refers to the conditions under which the dregs of society live as outcasts. The absence of effort leads not only to emptiness but to an undesirable lifestyle. Verses 32–34 underline the inescapable fact that the consequence of persistent idleness is poverty, which arrives with such suddenness and force that it cannot be resisted.

The picture is of a situation which has gone beyond repair. The wise do not let things get to this stage, but learn while there is time. These verses underline the urgency of the psalmist's words:

> O that today you would listen to his voice!
>> Do not harden your hearts... (Psalm 95:7–8).

TO THINK ABOUT

It is important to have high principles, but even more important to translate them into action, and this requires both help from God and effort on our part.

PRAYER

Lord, give me the will to think and do what is right, and the perseverance to continue in that way of life, and to resist boredom and discouragement.

SAYINGS *of the* KING

Hezekiah was king of Judah from about 715 to 687BC, and seems to have been a person of some literary ability (Isaiah 38:9–20). We cannot prove whether or not the dating given in verse 1 is correct, but if it is, it appears that Wisdom teaching was a matter of interest at court two centuries after Solomon. It seems unlikely that Hezekiah's court scribes spent their time copying ancient manuscripts; instead of 'copied' (which is an uncertain translation) we might read 'edited'. Every generation would have its scholars who both expanded previous material and wrote some of their own. So while chapters 25 and 26 in particular resemble the terse style of 10:1—22:16 (attributed to Solomon himself), they have their own characteristic ways of grouping ideas in rather longer passages—the courtiers (25:2–7), the fools (26:1, 3, 12), the lazybones (26:13–15) and the mischief-makers (26:17–28).

Kings and courtiers

In verses 2–7, the king is looked on favourably—there is a high view of his integrity and judgment (see also 16:10).

In verses 2 and 3, the ways of God and the king are both contrasted and compared. Each has his own 'glory', but whereas God's glory is in his inscrutable ways, the king's glory depends on his being *au fait* with what is going on, and his ability to identify and solve problems (v. 2). Yet just as the heavens are unreachable, so there is a place for mystery in the monarchy; the king (including any leader or head of state) must know how to keep his counsel (v. 3).

Verses 4 and 5 are about the realities of politics. As dross must be eliminated before a respectable silver vessel can be created (v. 4), so corruption must be rooted out before the throne can be secure and godly (v. 5). This is the desirable consequence of the king having his ear to the ground!

Verses 6 and 7 give some social advice about behaviour at Court. This setting is probably a feast: guests are allocated places according to rank or the king's favour, and it is unwise to assume an honoured position. In the New Testament, this situation is expanded into a parable which applies not to one occasion but to the whole of life:

When you are invited, go and sit down at the lowest place, so that when your host comes, he may say to you, 'Friend, move up higher'; then you will be honoured in the presence of all who sit at the table with you. For all who exalt themselves will be humbled, and those who humble themselves will be exalted (Luke 14:10–11).

Don't look a fool

The last line of verse 7 probably belongs to this section.

We need to be very sure that we know all the facts about a situation, and are able to interpret them correctly, before we embark on either a private or a legal dispute (v. 8). It is also wise and right to speak directly to whoever is involved with us in a difference of opinion, rather than talking to others about what should be confidential (v. 10). A hasty and ill-prepared argument makes us look foolish, and an indiscreet gossip is an object of contempt. This advice about desirability of a private settlement between the two people concerned anticipates the Sermon on the Mount: 'Come to terms quickly with your accuser while you are on the way to court with him, or your accuser may hand you over to the judge, and the judge to the guard, and you will be thrown into prison' (Matthew 5:25).

TO THINK ABOUT

At first sight, this passage seems to be mainly about appropriate behaviour in social and legal situations. But underlying the practical advice are the principles of discretion, integrity, humility, careful thought and plain speaking. All these are still essential if we are to conduct our lives in a godly way in today's society.

PRAYER

Lord, give me integrity, humility and generosity in all my dealings with others.

LIKE *to* LIKE (1)

A feature of chapters 25 and 26 is a series of comparisons; this is the first of several little groups, and it is about speech.

Like gold

'Apples' (v. 11) could mean quinces, apricots or oranges—all fragrant fruits. 'Gold' could describe the colour of the fruit, but probably means something valuable, typified by precious metal. The 'setting of silver' is sometimes translated 'baskets', but the word appears in Numbers 33:52 describing carved work. The overall impression is of the attractiveness and value of the appropriate spoken word; the gift of using words well benefits both speaker and hearer.

Verse 12 prizes equally the just word of rebuke. Here the benefit is to the hearer, provided he or she is prepared to listen. To be able to accept reproof is as valuable and attractive as the most costly ornament. The speaker is following in the tradition of Wisdom, who says, 'Give ear to my reproof' (1:23).

Like a cool drink

'Harvest' (v. 13) could last from March to September. It is unlikely that there would be snow during that time, so this probably means snow brought down from the mountains and kept in an underground ice-hole until it was needed. The point is that knowing we can rely on a messenger in a crisis is as welcome and reassuring as a cold drink to a hot and thirsty worker.

Like false signals

The 'gift' of which the speaker boasts (v. 14) is not a talent, but a promised present which never arrives, literally 'a gift of falsity'. Such unfulfilled promises bring the same kind of disappointment as clouds and wind which hold the hope of rain but never deliver.

Patience and determination

It seems surprising that patience towards a ruler is advised (v. 15). We would hardly expect an Old Testament king or ruler, who usually has great if not absolute power, to be susceptible to such an approach.

But quiet persistence can win surprising victories, as line two vividly—and figuratively—points out, softening and breaking down even the most resistant people (see also 15:1).

Knowing when to stop eating honey (v. 16) is an example of moderation: there is a difference between healthy enjoyment and greed. Self-control is held in high regard by the Wisdom writers (see comment on 17:27–28).

Another way of showing self-control (v. 17) is to be considerate of other people by restricting the number of uninvited visits we make and by not outstaying our welcome, otherwise friendship will be strained and the friend will become tired (literally 'sated') of our constant presence. This may seem a small thing, but good manners and sensitivity are important in Proverbs (see also v. 20).

Like to like (II)

The 'war club' (v. 18) means 'that which shatters'. The destructive metaphors used in verse 18 underline the seriousness of perjury, which is not only frequently condemned in Proverbs but expressly forbidden by the ninth Commandment: 'You shall not bear false witness against your neighbour' (Exodus 20:16).

Like a useless part of the body

Proverbs 18:24 condemns friends who are not serious about their commitment. Proverbs 25:19 goes further and deals with those who do not care enough to stand by someone in trouble. Like a rotten or broken tooth or a lame foot, they are useless. Just as they are 'faithless', so we are misguided if we put any faith in them.

Like acid on a sore

Vinegar has its uses, but when applied to a wound it is acutely painful. Cheerfulness has its place, but is acutely inappropriate when used in a misguided attempt to help someone in deep sorrow to 'snap out of it' (v. 20). Sadness is not dispelled in a moment, but there is a warning in the second half of the verse: if it is given a place for too long, it can be destructive. There is a word here for the sufferer as well as for the tactless friend.

PRAYER

Lord, help me to be sensitive and perceptive in all my relationships.

COALS *of* FIRE

The importance of treating our enemies (literally 'those who hate us') with kindness and restraint has already been spelled out in 20:22 and 24:17–18. 'Heaping coals of fire' (v. 22) can be understood in different ways: the shock of undeserved, unexpected kindness may bring the offender to contrition, or it may overwhelm them with shame and embarrassment—leading, one hopes, to the same result. Paul quotes these verses: 'If your enemies are hungry, feed them; if they are thirsty, give them something to drink; for by doing this you will heap burning coals on their heads' (Romans 12:20).

This particularly costly kindness brings a special reward from God (v. 22b)—presumably the satisfaction of knowing that we have acted obediently.

Unhappy relationships

The north wind in Palestine is usually a dry wind (v. 23) so either the reference is to the north-west wind, or the proverb comes from outside the country. However, the meaning is clear: just as a threatening wind brings rain, so malicious talk brings anger—no doubt from the person who is being maligned and perhaps from others. This and the sharp social comment in verse 24 (repeating 21:9) remind us of what we can do to other people by unkind words and behaviour.

Like to like (III)

Verse 25 takes the metaphor of verse 13 and applies it to different circumstances. At this time, anyone waiting for news, whether personal or professional, would have to wait weeks or even months, because communications are slow and uncertain. So there would be both impatience and anxiety. When news arrives and is good, the relief is overwhelming—like a cold drink to a parched throat. The joy of receiving good news is given a spiritual meaning by Isaiah:

> *How beautiful upon the mountains*
> *are the feet of the messenger who announces peace,*

who brings good news,
who announces salvation,
who says to Zion, 'Your God reigns' (Isaiah 52:7).

Like polluted water

This time, the drinking water is not welcome, but undrinkable (v. 26). 'Muddied' means literally 'trampled': sometimes animals or even people would walk into a fountain or pond, making it unfit to drink from. This contamination is like the corruption of someone or something good—a poison that spreads. When upright people compromise, those who respect and perhaps rely on them are affected for the worse.

Like an undefended city

When the walls of a fortified city are broken down, its defences are gone (v. 28). When we lose self-control, we are vulnerable to any emotion which attacks us. For the importance of self-control, see also verse 16, and 17:27–28.

More about excess

The first half of verse 27, like verse 16, describes eating honey, but here excess is compared to overwhelming ambition and seeking after prestige. The actual words are difficult to translate, but this seems to be the message.

TO THINK ABOUT

These verses are full of cause and effect: we have to live not only with things over which we have no control, like the slow system of communications in verse 25, but also with the consequences of our own thoughts and actions, both good and bad.

PRAYER

Lord, before I speak or act, may I remember that what I say or do will affect someone else.

LIKE *to* LIKE (IV)

This is the first part of what is sometimes called 'the Book of the Fool', because verses 1–12, with the exception of verse 2, all deal with those who are not only ignorant but also obstinate—they do not wish to learn wisdom.

Like unseasonable weather

The weather in Palestine was and is predictable: snow in summer and rain during the harvest season (see 25:13) are unheard of. In the same way, it is both unreasonable and incongruous to promote a stupid person to a post of responsibility (v. 1).

Like a bird flying harmlessly by

In the ancient world, blessings and curses were believed to be effective regardless of whether or not they were deserved. Here (v. 2), the unjustified curse is pictured as a bird fluttering ineffectively and getting nowhere—an idea which was the opposite of the usual belief. There is nothing to fear from ill-wishing when it is undeserved.

Like being immobilized

Sending a message by a fool is the equivalent of sending none at all. Such efforts lead nowhere—we might as well cut off our own legs (v. 6). 'Drinking down violence' must mean that by this misguided action we suffer violence, not that we inflict it.

How to handle the fool

An appeal to reason will not be effective (v. 3). Some commentators think that there is a contrast between the horse, used in warfare and hard to control, and the ass, favoured for riding, which needs much less severe discipline. Whether or not this is so, there is no doubt that the fool has to be dealt with firmly; subtlety is not the right treatment.

There may be a connection here with the psalmist's warning to those who resist God's guidance:

> I will instruct you and teach you the way you should go;
> I will counsel you with my eye upon you.

Do not be like a horse or a mule, without understanding,
  whose temper must be curbed with bit and bridle,
  else it will not stay near you (Psalm 32:8–9).

How to answer the fool

At first sight, the first lines of verses 4 and 5 seem to contradict each other; the rabbis took this view and even had some hesitations about regarding Proverbs as belonging to scripture. However, both sayings point out that there is no universal rule for solving problems. Sometimes it is best to speak to such people in their own terms so that at least we have tried to communicate, and sometimes it is best to say nothing in case they are confirmed in their foolishness. This is the constant dilemma of those who try to talk reasonably to those who are deaf to reason.

The fool tries to be clever

Such attempts fall disastrously flat (v. 7). The fool trying to invent a wise saying is as ineffective as someone paralysed trying to walk.

TO THINK ABOUT

The 'fool' in these verses is not someone who is mentally slow through no fault of their own, but the opposite of the 'wise', who live a life of reverent obedience to God. So although some of these verses have a sharp edge, and sound sarcastic at the expense of the dull and stupid, the people who are mocked are stupid not through inability but by their own wish: they do not wish to learn, and so become objects of derision. The underlying message of this passage is that wisdom and foolishness are not thrust upon us; they come as a result of our own choices.

LIKE *to* LIKE (V)

'The Book of the Fool' continues with four comparisons.

Like an incompetent practitioner

A stone is meant to be shot out of a sling. 'Binding it'—literally 'wrapping it up'—is ineffective; it can only be the action of someone who has no idea how a sling works. Verse 1 makes the point that to promote the fool is incongruous; here (v. 8) it is so useless as to be nonsensical. An even harsher interpretation is that the fool, like the stone, is meant to be got rid of, not retained and flattered.

Like a drunk with a stick

When fools attempt a wise saying, it is not only ineffective (see v. 7) but potentially harmful, because they do not know what to do with it and will misapply it (v. 9). The damage can be to the speaker or to others—it is both indiscriminate and irresponsible. There is a right way to convey sharp sayings, but it needs someone firm, authoritative and loving: 'The sayings of the wise are like goads, and like nails firmly fixed are the collected sayings that are given by one shepherd' (Ecclesiastes 12:11).

Like a careless employer

Verse 10 is almost impossible to translate; if we read it word for word it says something like 'Much wounds all, and he who hires a fool, and he who hires passers-by.' The one thing that seems clear is that it is about the folly of offering employment to people without finding out something about them—it is not only risky but possibly dangerous.

Like a dog's persistent habit

Fools never learn from experience; they go on making the same mistakes (v. 11). This saying is used in the New Testament in a slightly different way. It illustrates how even those who have some Christian understanding and experience can return to their former ways: 'It has happened to them according to the true proverb, "The dog turns back to its own vomit", and, "The sow is washed only to wallow in the mud"' (2 Peter 2:22).

Hope for the fool

After ten devastating verses, 'the Book of the Fool' ends with a glimmer of light (v. 12). There is someone even worse than the fool! A person who is full of conceit and self-aggrandisement may be intellectually able, but for that very reason is well defended against criticism. The fool, on the other hand, is obtuse, but not incapable of change. Only in this verse and 29:20 is the fool seen as anything but incurable.

'The Book of the Idle'

Verses 13–16 both emphasize and add to what has already been said in 6:6–11; 24:30–34 and elsewhere; they paint a witty but disturbing picture.

Lazy people can find every ridiculous reason for not going out (v. 13; see 22:13); the only time they exert themselves is when they turn over in bed—like the door, they move without going anywhere (v. 14). They are too 'tired' even to feed themselves (v. 15); certainly they cannot find the energy to finish a meal (see 19:24). Perhaps worst of all, they have no perception of their own mental indolence (v. 16). They are conceited like those in verse 12, and are under the impression that they are actually wiser than others ('seven' is a round number) who can talk sensibly.

TO THINK ABOUT

It could be quite demoralizing to read these verses; even though they do not describe us, there may be something in them which reminds us of ourselves. The verse which gives some cheer is verse 12: no one is beyond hope.

PRAYER

Lord, if any of this applies to me, I ask for your forgiveness and for the grace to put it right. I ask, too, for renewed hope and confidence.

LIKE *to* LIKE (VI)

Verses 17–22 are all about mischief-making and the damage it can do both to the perpetrators and to the victims.

Like a foolish taker of risks

'To meddle' can mean 'to get excited'. Of course there are times when help is needed and asked for, but as a rule we get no thanks for interfering in other people's quarrels—we are more likely to find the anger turned on us, just as the dog will resent any attempt at control by a stranger. The New Testament has some words of warning for people who positively make a career out of involvement in the affairs of others: 'We hear that some of you are living in idleness, mere busybodies, not doing any work. Now such persons we command and exhort in the Lord Jesus Christ to do their work quietly and to earn their own living' (2 Thessalonians 3:11–12).

'Only joking'

To deceive someone, and then use the escape clause 'I was only in fun', is not funny (vv. 18–19). It is irresponsible as well as hurtful, and can do as much damage as a maniac in possession of deadly weapons.

Malicious gossip

This is malice, not the idle gossip of 11:13. The writer gives us two pictures to illustrate its effects. First, the fire. The 'whisperer' who opens the conversation with 'I thought you ought to know', and the quarrelsome person, between them, keep talk and rumour going, just as charcoal and wood stoke up a fire (v. 21). If the source of the gossip dries up, it all dies away, like the fire which is fed no more fuel (v. 20).

Second, there is the pleasurable side of gossip (v. 22)—like delicious titbits which reach our innermost parts and, like unwholesome food, do us no good (see 18:8).

Like to like (VII)

The 'glaze' (v. 23) can be deceptive, since the word can also mean 'silver of dross'—that is, an impure mixture which can overlay pottery and give the impression of real silver. Whichever translation we use, the picture is of a deceptively attractive surface concealing something mean and specious, just like the words of a hypocrite.

The next three verses develop this thought. The 'enemy' must mean the person who, perhaps unbeknown to the victim, is full of hatred. This ill-feeling can be disguised by words just as the inferior pottery is disguised by the glaze (v. 24) but we should be alert in trying to spot it, and more than cautious about believing the kind words which conceal an indefinite number of unacceptable thoughts (v. 25).

In the end, we have to believe with verse 26 that evil will be exposed and judged, whether in the formal sense or by public opinion. The 'assembly' can mean an informal gathering of citizens or it may be the Jewish civic organizations which in the later Old Testament were given the right to administer justice.

The biter bit

Mischief recoils on the mischief maker (v. 27). The pit, presumably dug with malicious intent, and the stone, presumably rolled uphill so that it will roll back and crush, will one day do the same to the one who is responsible for them.

Summing up the whole matter

Lying and insincerity often conceal hatred towards their victims and bring ruin on both them and their persecutors. Truth is the vital ingredient in every situation (v. 28).

TO THINK ABOUT

Like the rest of the chapter, this passage has some hard sayings. The positive side of what it has to say is the importance of integrity and sincerity. While meddling, malice and untruths bring misery, discretion, kindness and openness are the foundation of good relationships.

OVER-CONFIDENCE

In the early part of this chapter we revert to single, brief sayings, sometimes loosely connected, sometimes standing alone.

It is stating the obvious to say that we can never be sure what will happen on any day (v. 1). We need to beware of an optimism which comes from the feeling that we can handle anything, and which is geared to selfish plans: 'Come now, you who say, "Today or tomorrow we will go to such and such a town and spend a year there doing business and making money" ... Instead, you ought to say, "If the Lord wishes, we will live and do this or that"' (James 4:13, 15).

The opposite tendency is to worry unduly, and this is addressed in the Sermon on the Mount: 'Do not worry about tomorrow, for tomorrow will bring worries of its own. Today's trouble is enough for today' (Matthew 6:34).

Nor is boasting about ourselves and our achievements to be recommended; leave that to someone else (v. 2). The only praise that matters is God's approval; we do not need to tell him about our good deeds and piety, for 'your Father who sees in secret will reward you' (Matthew 6:4, 6, 18).

Uncomfortable emotions

Fools have no sense of proportion, so when a fool provokes us or is angry, it is unreasonably heavy and burdensome (v. 3). Ben Sirach, the writer of Ecclesiasticus in the Apocrypha, gives much the same sense of weight and weariness:

> Sand, salt, and a lump of iron
> are less of a burden than a stupid man (Ecclesiasticus 22:15, NEB).

Anger can be overwhelming (v. 4, literally 'a flood'), but usually the storm passes. Jealousy is something else—more cruel, more persistent, more corrosive, and very difficult to control. In scripture, there is jealousy for someone or something in the sense of hatred of what is wrong: 'Thus says the Lord of hosts: I am jealous for Zion with great jealousy, and I am jealous for her with great wrath' (Zechariah 8:2).

But jealousy of someone or something is 'fierce as the grave' (see Song of Solomon 8:6, where 'passion' is the same word as 'jealousy'); it can have something of the cold finality of death.

Honest friendship

Real love is open: it does not shrink from speaking out when something is wrong either with the friend or the situation (v. 5).

'Faithful are the wounds of a friend' (v. 6, KJV) has become a familiar saying in English. 'Faithfulness', or reliability and stability, is an attribute which belongs to our relationship with God as well as with each other; it may be costly, but we are commanded to hold it fast (see 3:3). By contrast, the person who is profuse with indiscriminate praise and affection does us no service.

Hunger is the best sauce?

At first sight this looks like the meaning of verse 7, but there are other ways of reading it. It may be saying that our reactions in general depend on our circumstances, or it may mean that we spurn (or 'trample on') sweet talk when we have had a surfeit of it, but are glad of it when we rarely get it. Of the three possible interpretations the first, which is the most straightforward, seems the most likely.

TO THINK ABOUT

How many of these raw emotions do we feel? And are we prepared to pay the price of true friendship by speaking and receiving the truth without resentment?

PRAYER

Lord, show me how to deal with pride and jealousy and my need for satisfaction and affirmation.

HOME TIES

The word for 'home' (v. 8) means literally 'place'. The need for a sense of place within a family or a community is strong in us all, and was particularly so in the ancient Near East. 'Stray' reads like wilful desertion, but in fact it is a neutral word, meaning 'wander'. Any withdrawal from the security of our roots, whether because of business, eviction, vagrancy or estrangement, can make us feel literally like 'displaced persons'. Roots are important. If we interpret this verse in a Christian context, it emphasizes that our unfailing security is when we are 'rooted and built up in (Christ) and established in the faith' (Colossians 2:7).

Things that really matter

We can choose between two meanings for verse 9. If, like the NRSV, we follow the Greek Old Testament, it is contrasting the pleasure and soothing effect of perfumes with the lacerating effect of trouble. If we follow the Hebrew, the second half of the verse says, 'The sweetness of a friend is better than one's own counsel'. This compares the perfumes with the soothing effect of friendship, but 'better than one's own counsel' is not so easy to understand. Perhaps it means that just as perfumes are applied externally, we benefit from the advice and support of someone other than ourselves.

The advice in the first part of verse 10 is to stick with old friends of the family, rather than dropping them for new and perhaps more exciting company. Ahikar, writing in Assyria in the seventh century BC, says:

> *My son, remove not thy father's friend,*
> *lest perchance thy friend come not near thee.*

The last part states the obvious—Ahikar again points out:

> *My son, better is a friend at hand*
> *than a brother who is far away.*

The advice 'not to go to the house of your kindred in the day of your calamity' is not easy to understand. Although in 18:24 it is admitted that sometimes a true friend is even more faithful than family, 17:17 makes the point that both friends and relatives are there to see us through hard times. If this central section of the verse is part of the original, the 'house of your kindred' must be the place which is too far away to go to for help.

The responsible teacher

Whether this is a parent or a wisdom teacher addressing 'my child' (v. 11), they are held responsible for the faults of the child or pupil. Quite apart from their interest in the student's welfare, they look for the pleasure which successful teaching brings, and hope to escape the insults which follow failure.

Two verses repeated

Verses 12 and 13 are the same as 22:3 and 20:16. At a time when printing was unknown, and writing was both slow and expensive, the 'officials of King Hezekiah' (25:1) must have thought that warnings about prudence in times of danger and caution in taking pledges were important enough to be given more than once.

The over-hearty friend

Verse 14 continues what has been said in 25:17 and 20 about the intrusive neighbour and the tactless acquaintance. For one thing, loud salutations early in the morning are not likely to be welcome; for another, there is no guarantee that these attentions are genuine (see v. 6). This trio of sayings about inappropriate speech and behaviour is a sharp reminder that even friends need some space and privacy.

PRAYER

Lord, may I always be loyal to my friends and sensitive to their needs. And help me to remember with gratitude my parents and teachers, and to practise the good things which they taught me.

GOOD & BAD EXCHANGES

The nagging wife (vv. 15–16) is a character we have met before (see 19:13). Here, however, it is not only her wearying and exasperating effect on others which is described (v. 15), it is the fact that humanly speaking she cannot be controlled. The general sense of verse 16 is that it is impossible either to contain (literally 'hide') or restrain someone who is as unpredictable as the wind and as slippery as oil.

Is there no hope of resolving this sad situation? Certainly the writer gives none, but this is one of the occasions on which he simply states a fact, rather than offering instruction or advice.

In verse 17, the writer may be thinking in the first place of the intellectual conversations between teachers and students, but it is a fact that friendship, like education, should be not only enjoyable and supportive (17:17) but also bracing and stimulating. Part of development is learning to listen and to differ without quarrelling.

Faithful service

The idea of serving others (v. 18) is commended in Proverbs (see 22:29). Anyone who 'takes care of' or 'has due regard to' their employer's interests—that is, who gives loyal service—is promised the same sure reward as the gardener who tends a fig tree and can expect to eat its fruit. This is about human service; but the New Testament makes the same point about serving God: 'Do your best to present yourself to God as one approved by him, a worker who has no need to be ashamed, rightly explaining the word of truth' (2 Timothy 2:15).

Knowing yourself

The simplest way to understand verse 19 is to take it that we see our own virtues and faults by observing other people. Another possible meaning is that we understand ourselves by examining our reflections in water as we would in a mirror. To try to see ourselves clearly takes courage and determination—we may not like what we see.

Never satisfied

Sheol and Abaddon (v. 20) have already appeared in 1:12 and 15:11.

They are never satisfied: the long procession of human beings that they swallow up nowhere near fills them.

In the same way, human desires are insatiable. The eye appears as a symbol of desire in Ecclesiastes 4:8: 'Their eyes are never satisfied with riches.'

Humanly speaking, there is no answer to this dissatisfaction; however, the New Testament points to a different solution: 'Jesus said to her, "Everyone who drinks of this water will be thirsty again, but those who drink of the water that I will give them will never be thirsty"' (John 4:13–14).

Proving one's mettle

It is necessary to test the purity of metals; it is equally essential to test a person's character. How can we do this? The second part of verse 21 may simply mean that we assess people by their reputation (though public opinion is by no means always right). Or we can take it that praise, even more than persecution, is the true test of character. When we are praised, do we become self-important? Do we take ourselves at other people's valuation? Or are we mature enough to be grateful for the appreciation we receive while remaining realistic about it?

The word used in verse 22 for 'fool' implies a person of moral insolence; the folly is not an isolated moral lapse, but a matter of character and intellect. Unless it is dealt with early in life (22:15) it is difficult if not impossible to eradicate. This verse takes an even more gloomy view about the incorrigibility of the foolish person than 26:3.

TO THINK ABOUT

What is the answer to the perpetual dissatisfaction in human nature? Humanly speaking, there is none, but read verse 20 again. Augustine, Bishop of Hippo from 396 to 430, wrote: 'Thou hast made us for thyself, and our hearts are restless till they rest in thee.'

COUNTRY LIFE

We switch from the city and the Court to the country, with some hints on how to make a satisfactory living from farming.

Verses 23 and 24 give the basic instruction: 'Take care of (have regard to) your animals, and use your resources prudently, because wealth, whether in money or in livestock, does not last for ever.' The land in Palestine was and is more suited to raising flocks than to growing crops, and although oxen are mentioned elsewhere in Proverbs (14:4; 15:17), the terrain seems to have been good for rearing smaller animals such as sheep and goats. Verse 25 describes the two growths of grass: that on the plains, which is cut and used for hay, and that on high pasture land, which also yields some fodder.

Prudent management results in sufficient clothing, profit and food (vv. 26–27) for a whole household, not forgetting the humblest servants.

An idyllic picture

What has this to say to the young who are being trained as courtiers and diplomats? And what has it to say to us at the beginning of the twenty-first century?

First of all, there was not the gap between town and country life in ancient Palestine that there is in our society, and noblemen were quite likely to be responsible for, and dependent upon, rural estates, which might serve them better than any, probably temporary, advantage they might gain at Court. Now, as then, there is an obligation to manage property with care and thought for those who are dependent on us. Nowhere does the Bible approve the irresponsible squandering of assets.

Second, there is a sharp reminder of the temporary nature of riches (v. 24). There is no guarantee that they will last, and one day we shall have to leave them behind (for 'crown' read 'wealth', since it was the firm belief that the dynasty of David would last for ever!) 'If riches increase, do not set your heart on them' (Psalm 62:10).

In the New Testament, we are taught that riches, and the importance we attach to them, can actually be a hindrance to entering God's kingdom: 'It is easier for a camel to go through the eye of a

needle than for someone who is rich to enter the kingdom of God'
(Mark 10:25).

Third, we can apply these verses more widely. They remind us that we are living in God's created world, and that we must treat it appropriately. It is there for our use and pleasure, but not to be taken for granted or despoiled selfishly. We must be good stewards of what has been entrusted to us.

TO THINK ABOUT

Sometimes as Christians we concentrate on the redeeming love of God in Christ, and neglect the importance of his work in creation. The psalmist reminds us:

'The earth is the Lord's and all that is in it,
the world, and those who live in it;
for he has founded it on the seas,
and established it on the rivers.'
(Psalm 24:1–2)

PRAYER

Lord, may we remember that we are your creation, and live with loving gratitude and thoughtful lifestyles in the world which is yours.

SOCIAL JUSTICE

In chapter 28 there is from time to time an emphasis on social justice, particularly as it affects the treatment of the poor and underprivileged. Links are also made (vv. 5, 9, 25) between the fulfilment of these responsibilities and spiritual well-being.

To be expected

A guilty conscience often means looking anxiously over our shoulders (v. 1); a clear conscience, on the other hand, means being able to walk through life with the confidence of a young lion and having nothing to fear.

Although the Hebrew of verse 2 is not very clear, the gist of it is that restlessness and rebellion in a nation lead to instability, possibly even to civil war between rival rulers. In just over two centuries, until it was overrun by Assyria in 721BC, the Northern Kingdom of Israel had nine monarchs, and all except the first came to power after an assassination.

A devastating tyranny

Verse 3 has two possible meanings. If we take the NRSV translation it refers to a cruel and powerful tyrant; but if we translate literally, it begins 'A poor person who oppresses the poor…'. It is in keeping with the thought of Proverbs to be vigilant about oppressive rulers, and it may seem unlikely that the poor would have the means to persecute their equals. But if they are able to do so in any way, the misery they impose has the added bitterness of betrayal. It is like the unseasonable rain which, unusually for Palestine, brings havoc and deprivation. There is something particularly harmful and hurtful about ill-treatment by our peers.

Two views of ethics

Whether the 'law' here (v. 4) means the code of morality laid down in the first five books of the Bible (see 13:13) or the framework of every aspect of Jewish life, or whether it refers to the teaching of godly parents (see 1:8), our attitude to it affects our attitude to others. If we believe in an absolute moral code, we wage war against wickedness;

if we deny it, everything is relative and it is much harder to condemn, and much easier to condone, anything and anybody.

Spiritual blindness and spiritual understanding

Wickedness and injustice (v. 5), as often in Proverbs, are associated with (probably deliberate) ignorance and unconcern. True seekers after God will learn his will, and be guided into insight and awareness of how justice works:

I understand more than the aged,
for I keep your precepts (Psalm 119:100).

Honest poverty and doubtful wealth

The first part of verse 6 is the same as that of 19:1, describing those who are upright although they might understandably be tempted to be otherwise. The second line contrasts them favourably with some rich people whose ways are, to say the least of it, questionable.

Wise and foolish offspring

Here again in verse 7, as in verse 4, 'law' may be interpreted in two ways. But the attitude of the young will either bring wisdom or lead them into the wrong company—'gluttons', or spendthrifts—with resulting shame for their parents. This echoes more succinctly the thoughts of 23:19–25.

TO THINK ABOUT

These verses offer choices and require decisions. For example, is
there anything on our consciences that we ought to deal with? Do
we treat others with kindness and justice? Do we belive that right
and wrong are absolutes, or do they depend on our own ideas?
Does our financial state affect our integrity? How do we react to
our children's lifestyles? We need God's help in resolving these and
other vital questions.

The DOWNSIDE *of* BEING WEALTHY

Wealth can bring greed (v. 8). Charging interest on a loan was forbidden by the Law with the exception of loans to 'strangers', or foreigners (Deuteronomy 23:19–20). In those days money was as a rule lent—not, as now, for commercial reasons—but to supply the poor with the bare necessities of life. The same rule applied throughout the ancient world, but nobody found any means of enforcing it, as Nehemiah discovered among the returned exiles in Jerusalem: 'I brought charges against the nobles and the officials; I said to them, "You are all taking interest from your own people"' (Nehemiah 5:7).

'Exorbitant interest' is literally 'interest and usury'; and charging such rates will end in loss of wealth, either through divine judgment or because of social disapproval. The money will somehow come into the hands of someone who will use it in a humane way (see 14:31).

Wealth can also lead to excessive self-importance (v. 11). However, anyone of intelligence, who may be in a less advantageous social position, can see through this and is not impressed. Complacency does not commend itself, even if it is backed by a lot of money and possessions.

Trying to have it both ways

We must first listen, whether it is to the law or to the teaching of wisdom (see vv. 4, 7) and then obey. Attempts to pray when we are heedless of and disobedient to God's commands (v. 9) are uncomfortable for us and wholly unacceptable to him—they are 'an abomination' (see 15:8).

Corruption and integrity

Verse 10 takes a realistic view of human nature. The 'upright' are as susceptible to undesirable influences as anyone else—perhaps even more so because they may have a certain innocence. To encourage them or anyone else into wrong attitudes or ways will be counterproductive, and recoil on the perpetrator (see 26:27). Those with a clear conscience, on the other hand, have nothing to fear, as we see in verse 1.

Two states of the nation

When power comes into the hands of the upright (literally, 'when the righteous rejoice'—presumably meaning 'give cause for rejoicing' by coming into government), there is happiness and prosperity. When there is an oppressive regime, people suffer and may even be driven into hiding.

This thought in verse 12 is similar to those expressed in 11:10 and 14:34: national well-being depends on godly leadership.

Concealment and confession

Verse 13 is the only verse in Proverbs where confession is mentioned, though it figures largely in the rest of the Bible. Hiding our faults means living a lie, and does us no good. However, acknowledging them—even, in the Old Testament setting, with the accompaniment of sacrifice—is not enough. True repentance means change:

> For you have no delight in sacrifice;
>   if I were to give a burnt offering, you would not be pleased.
> The sacrifice acceptable to God is a broken spirit;
>   a broken and a contrite heart, O God, you will not despise
>
>   (Psalm 51:16–17).

Reverence and arrogance

Are we really intended to be haunted by fear, as at first sight verse 14 implies? The answer is 'No'; 'fear'—a strong word which we might translate 'great awe'—is used in the sense of 'godfearing', implying a healthy respect for what is right and for the One who sets these standards. In contrast, the brazen attitude of someone who is without this restraint is likely to lead to disaster of one kind or another.

√ PRAYER

Lord, show me how both to love and to fear you.

The OPPRESSIVE RULER

Verses 15 and 16 paint a depressing picture of the mindless tyrant, crashing about like a wild animal (v. 15), and of the one who may be less noisy but has no more intelligence or discernment (v. 16). The writer does not spell out the future of either of these, but we infer that since the honest ruler will enjoy long life, the long-term prospects for the oppressor must be correspondingly poor: he may suffer a miserable life or an early death. This may feel like small consolation to those who are being exploited, but it is in line with the teaching throughout Proverbs.

The price of conscience

Verse 17 is unusual because it is not poetry; although it is set out in poetic form, it is actually a single sentence making its point without either contrast or repetition, so it may have been inserted into Proverbs from another source. It is less unusual in that a literal translation makes little sense! It reads, 'One who is burdened with another person's blood will flee to a pit; let them not grasp him.'

A picture emerges of someone desperate after committing a crime—perhaps murder, perhaps a lesser offence—carrying a weight of guilt and trying desperately to escape. It could be that the destination is one of the designated 'cities of refuge' where an accidental killer could be safe (Numbers 35:22–25). Perhaps part of the punishment for the offender is that they are to be neither apprehended nor helped, but must carry their burden all their life. Here we are warned against interfering with justice; in 24:11–12 we are told that we must not be indifferent to suffering—two sides of the same coin.

Those who live an upright life need fear nothing (see v. 1). But those whose lifestyle is crooked or devious will come to grief (v. 18). 'The Pit' is not Sheol; the actual words say 'will fall (all) at once', perhaps meaning 'one way or another'. 'Ways' actually implies 'two ways', so it may be that the downfall comes from trying to live a double life, which cannot be sustained.

Time well spent and time wasted

There is a choice between two kinds of plenty (v. 19). Plenty of produce for the diligent workers; plenty of poverty for those who waste their lives on trivial and profitless affairs. The work ethic is strong in Proverbs—see also 12:11.

Verses 20 and 22 are about priorities. Those who put their own ambition and greed first (v. 20) will fail and in some way come to a bad end—perhaps because in their hurry they have used dishonest methods, for which they suffer the penalty. Those who are even more set on money (v. 22) (literally 'who have an evil eye', meaning being greedy and grasping—see 23:6) have not even time to contemplate their inner poverty until it is too late. By contrast, the 'faithful' or trustworthy (v. 20) will reap the rewards of honest work. The New Testament has something to say about the consequences of avarice: 'Those who want to be rich fall into temptation and are trapped by many senseless and harmful desires that plunge people into ruin and destruction' (1 Timothy 6:9).

Verse 21, like other verses in Proverbs (for example, 18:5 and 24:23), deals with corruption in the law courts. While it repeats that there must be absolute impartiality, it adds that it is frightening to think what a small bribe will do.

TO THINK ABOUT

There is a lot in these verses about the misuse of power, the misuse of time, and the misuse of ambition. It is helpful sometimes to think about our goals and our priorities, and to ask ourselves whether these are in line with God's ways and character.

PRAYER

You are indeed my rock and my fortress;
for your name's sake lead me and guide me.
(Psalm 31:3)

The BEST POLICY

Verse 23 reinforces 27:5–6 by commending plain speaking, but it also looks at the later benefits of such candour. At the time, flattery is gratifying and reproof hard to take, but with hindsight it is often the honest opinion which is remembered with gratitude.

Dishonesty is degrading

'Robbing' parents (v. 24), in the society of the time, might mean swindling them by some shady deal to do with the family property—not too difficult in the extended family. We can hear the self-deluding words: 'They don't need it', 'It will be mine one day anyway', 'They would want me to have it', 'It's all in the family', and so on.

Any such practice brings the child to the level of a thug. According the *Oxford English Dictionary*, the thug is a 'cut-throat' or 'ruffian'; the Hebrew word means 'a wrecker'. This sort of unscrupulous behaviour towards parents breaks the fifth Commandment to 'honour your father and your mother' (Exodus 20:12) and places its perpetrator beneath contempt. It is in sad contrast to the respectful attitude to the older generation which is urged in 23:22.

Greed and arrogance

Greedy people (REB has 'grasping') (v. 25) always cause trouble—jealousy between others and hostility towards themselves. By contrast, those who are humble and not self-seeking (because their security is in God) are likely to flourish. Jesus says: 'Strive first for the kingdom of God and his righteousness, and all these things will be given to you as well' (Matthew 6:33).

The arrogant are also condemned (v. 26). Those who think themselves brilliant are inevitably foolish—they should leave that judgment to others—and the prospects for the fool are not good. But the 'wise', who have learnt that 'the fear of the Lord is the beginning of wisdom', will use their God-given intelligence to deal with any situation which may arise. The New Testament also stresses the need for humility; for example: 'Do not be haughty, but associate with the lowly; do not claim to be wiser than you are' (Romans 12:16).

Giving and getting

The teaching that generosity will actually ensure prosperity (v. 27) is not new to the reader of Proverbs (see 11:24–26 and 22:9), but here, something is promised for those who are too mean-spirited to want to know about the needy. Whether the 'curse' comes from God himself or from the poor, the assumption is that it will have the power to blight its recipient's life.

Fear and liberty

Verse 28 echoes the thought of verse 12, but it emphasizes the downfall of the oppressive regime rather than the inauguration of good government. One of the terrifying results of oppression is the need for people to hide from persecution. This is not peculiar to the time of Proverbs; it happens all over the world at any time, including the present. The unspoken message must be to work for the liberation of those who suffer, so that the 'increase of the righteous' may become a reality.

TO THINK ABOUT

Most of these verses repeat or enlarge on what has already been said, so they need to be taken especially seriously. One of the most searching is verse 24. How do we treat the older generation—with respect or with an amused tolerance bordering on contempt? Are we strictly honourable if we have any responsibility for administering their property? Can we make sure that we shall not have to deal with regrets at some later time, perhaps when it is our turn to be dependent on others?

PRAYER

Lord, give me grace and patience in my dealings with older family and friends. Help me to give them the honour and respect which you command us to give.

BETTER *to* BEND *than to* BREAK

'To be stubborn' (v. 1) is literally 'to harden one's neck'—a picture of unyielding rigidity which we have already met in 1:24–33 and will meet again in the New Testament, when Stephen says to the Jewish leaders, 'You stiff-necked people... you are for ever opposing the Holy Spirit, just as your ancestors used to do' (Acts 7:51).

This attitude can continue for a long time, then suddenly there will be a disaster which cannot be put right—the more shattering because its pig-headed victim has not been expecting it.

More about government

This is important to the 'the officials of King Hezekiah', since it has already been mentioned twice in chapter 28 (vv. 12 and 28). Here, there is the same contrast (v. 2) between the rule of the righteous and that of the wicked, but there is an additional comment about the responsibility of the king (v. 4). It was accepted that the king had the right to levy taxes, but sometimes this could become heavy and oppressive, especially if the money was used, as in the reign of Solomon, to finance magnificent building projects or foreign wars. Small wonder that when Solomon's son said, 'My father made your yoke heavy, but I will add to your yoke', the nation of Israel was split, never to be re-united (1 Kings 12:14).

By contrast, Hezekiah is one of the few kings of whom it is said, 'He did what was right in the sight of the Lord' (2 Kings 18:3). His officials, having had experience of just rule, make it a priority in the sayings which they choose for editing.

Children wise and foolish

The child who lives wisely is a continuing joy to the parents (see, for example, 10:1; 23:15–16, 24; 27:11). This time (v. 3), the problem offspring is not the one who cheats the older generation (see 28:24) but the one who, in rejecting wisdom, becomes promiscuous—a sad state of affairs dealt with at length in chapters 1—9. 'Squander' may refer literally to the financial consequences of wrongdoing (see 5:10; 6:31) or to the wanton rejection of the parents' love.

Two kinds of snare

Self-esteem is ridiculously inflated by flattery (see 26:28; 28:23), which, ironically, is usually untrue (the word for 'flatter' carries also a sense of guile and deceit). The recipient becomes entangled in it—perhaps addicted to it (v. 5).

A more general snare is that by which sin of any kind traps the sinner (v. 6)—it is easier to get into evil ways than to get out of them. The righteous, on the other hand, (to translate literally) 'run and rejoice'—not because the wicked have fallen into their own trap, but because they are free to live without fear.

Justice for the poor

The righteous 'know'—that is, have a personal concern for (see 12:10)—the justice legally due to the poor, presumably because they have taken the trouble to find out (v. 7). One does not need to be actively cruel or oppressive to be classified as 'wicked' in this context; it is enough to take the attitude of 'not wanting to know'.

Rabble-rousers and peacemakers

We have met the 'scoffers' many times before in Proverbs (see 1:22; 9:7–8; 14:6; 21:24 and 24:9), so we know that they are among the hardest cases, with their arrogance and contempt for morality. Here (v. 8), their vindictiveness is inflammatory: they fan the flames of discontent (literally 'puff out words') until a town is alight with rebellion. The wise, on the other hand, work to defuse anger; like all peacemakers they may not achieve spectacular immediate results but it is by their efforts that passions are cooled and order is restored.

When the wise are foolish

Never go to law with a fool (v. 9); there is no sense in arguing, for fools cannot be objective, and the result will be a lot of noise and no solution. Far better to cut your losses.

PRAYER

Lord, these verses are full of foolish and stubborn people. Please give me your wisdom; help me to avoid falling into these sins myself, and to speak out when I see other people suffering because of them.

101 PROVERBS 29:10–18

PUBLIC ORDER

The violent (literally 'men of blood') have no cause to wish well those of integrity—who are literally 'together'. Perhaps there is an unacknowledged feeling of jealousy.

The meaning of the second part of verse 10 is not entirely clear. The REB has 'they (the upright) see to their interests'—that is, the interests of the bloodthirsty. This would be in line with 25:21–22, which urges kindness to our enemies. However, this verse is not an instruction but a description of what happens, and it makes more sense to take the NRSV translation, particularly as 'to seek someone's life' is used elsewhere in the Old Testament in a hostile sense. Elijah says, 'I alone am left, and they are seeking my life, to take it away' (1 Kings 19:10).

In verse 11, 'anger' means 'mind' or 'spirit'—describing the uncontrolled expression of our thoughts. Proverbs 16:32 and 25:28 praise self-restraint and condemn the lack of it, but 'holds it back' means more than repressing anger: it is the word used in Psalm 89:9 of God stilling the storm, and suggests overcoming as well as checking.

There are two thoughts in verse 12. First, the person in charge, whether royal or not, must exercise discernment as to the truth or otherwise of what they are told (see 16:10; 20:8 where this applies to the king). Second, a regime where truth is not valued rapidly becomes corrupt—flattery and lies do their work.

In verse 14, the king is directly mentioned (see also v. 4 and 16:12). The stability of the throne depends on the right administration of justice, particularly towards those members of society who are in no position to put pressure on the authorities.

Proverbs 22:2 gave a reminder that all of us, rich and poor, are God's creatures; verse 13 goes further. The oppressor and the oppressed share the privilege of enjoying his creation. Jesus makes this a reason for treating each other with equality (Matthew 5:44–45).

Discipline and neglect

We know the benefits of loving but firm discipline in the family (see,

216

for example, 13:24; 23:13–14), but the dangers of neglect are addressed here (v. 15). Children who are (literally) 'sent away' because nobody can be bothered with them are unlikely to be a credit to their parents. The mother is singled out here, perhaps because she has most to do with the training of the young child. On the other hand, where there is training and correction (v. 17), children can 'give rest'—that is, relieve us of anxiety rather than being an anxiety—and can be a delight—something to be enjoyed.

The end of the matter

Verse 16 repeats the thought of 28:12, 28 and of verse 2, and carries it further: nothing, not even an evil and corrupt government, will last for ever. The psalmist prays for endurance in situations of this sort:

> Be merciful to me, O God, be merciful to me,
>   for in you my soul takes refuge;
> in the shadow of your wings I will take refuge,
>   until the destroying storms pass by (Psalm 57:1–2).

Living without God

Prophecy is God's direct word; together with the Law and the Wisdom writings such as Proverbs, it makes up a great part of the Old Testament. Both Law and Prophecy are necessary for general order and happiness; without both, nothing can prevent people (here in verse 18, people in general, not the nation) from running wild. Earlier, at a time when public morality was at a low ebb, 'the word of the Lord was rare in those days; visions were not widespread' (1 Samuel 3:1).

TO THINK ABOUT

Read verse 18 again, and consider how far it applies to today's society. Are we living without reference to God's law? And where are the prophets who can say with authority, 'This is what the Lord says'? Are we ignoring them, or are they not to be found?

PRAYER

Lord, may I be a faithful witness to you, even though it means holding unfashionable and unpopular views.

HASTY WORDS, BAD TEMPER

In the culture of the time, a responsible and co-operative slave could even take the place of an unsatisfactory child (see 17:2). However, here the situation is one where a servant is irresponsible and, perhaps wilfully, stupid (v. 19). The implication is that mere words will not be enough; the discipline must be as severe as that applied to the children in the family (see v. 17 and 9:7; 19:18). In the same way, where the master is foolishly indulgent (v. 21) the outcome will be, to say the least of it, unsatisfactory. The KJV interprets the rather difficult Hebrew as 'will find him his heir', that is, usurping the place of the real heir; the REB has 'he will prove ungrateful'.

Only verse 20 and 26:12 give some hope for the fool—because there are people even worse! In 26:12 it is the arrogant person who cannot or will not face up to the need for change; here it is anyone who speaks without thinking—the ultimate folly.

Verse 22 is not about an isolated incident, but describes those who are habitually ill-tempered. This fault breeds quarrelling and brings more wrongdoing (probably the author is thinking of feuds and recriminations) in its wake. Proverbs 14:17, 29; 15:18 and 22:24–25 make the same point.

High and low

Pride (see 16:18–19) does not bring honour but ends in humiliation (literally 'being brought low'), while genuine humility, which characterizes those who are 'lowly in spirit' (the play on words is not obvious in English), leads to true esteem (v. 23). The same thought appears in the New Testament, when Mary the mother of Jesus says:

He has scattered the proud in the thoughts of their hearts.
He has brought down the powerful from their thrones,
   and lifted up the lowly (Luke 1:51–52).

Trouble and true security

Two things are the matter in verse 24. First, anyone who has dealings with a thief is his or her own worst enemy. Second, this sort of association may lead to keeping silence in a court of law when one ought to speak. Whether what one hears is the victim's 'curse' (or oath), or the instruction to speak, there is a duty under the Law to give evidence: 'When any of you sin in that you have heard a public adjuration to testify and—though able to testify... —does not speak up, you are subject to punishment' (Leviticus 5:1).

Fear, whether it is general apprehension or the fear of what other people will say or think, is a powerful and crippling emotion (v. 25). The way of release is to put our trust in God, who will give the security we long for (literally 'set us on high', above such concerns; see 18:10).

The same problem appears in a different guise in verse 26. This time, the anxiety shows itself in seeking 'the face' of a ruler—perhaps meaning trying to insist on an audience with him, or some other form of recognition. Kings and rulers are expected to be just (see 16:10), but over-reliance on them is misplaced; the unfailing source of justice is God.

Total incompatibility

'An abomination' usually describes something which God hates (see comment on 24:9), but here (v. 27) the wicked and the upright equally detest each other; they have, or at least should have, nothing whatsoever in common.

TO THINK ABOUT

The last five chapters, the 'other proverbs of Solomon that the officials of King Hezekiah of Judah copied' (25:1), have often repeated what has already been said, and sometimes have expressed it even more strongly. These thoughts were of great importance to those who selected and edited them; re-read them and think how they apply to your life.

PRAYER

Open my eyes, so that I may behold wondrous things out of your law.
(Psalm 119:18)

INTRODUCING AGUR

He is not easy to introduce. First, Agur and Jakeh (v. 1) are not Hebrew names, and 'oracle' can also be translated 'Massa' (so RSV)— a place possibly in northern Arabia—in which case 'Agar son of Jakeh of Massa' confirms that this is a non-Israelite piece of writing. Second, if we stay with 'oracle' it is still an unusual word, because it generally refers to prophecy rather than to Wisdom sayings of this kind. Third, by altering the consonants of 'I am weary, O God. How can I prevail?' we have 'The man says to Ithiel, to Ithiel and Ucal' (RSV); but as we know nothing about these two people we are probably best to keep to the NRSV! What this amounts to is that we do not know who wrote this chapter, but we do learn quite a lot about him.

The author—whether genuinely or ironically—laments his stupidity and lack of discernment (v. 2), particularly his lack of the 'fear of the Lord' which is 'the beginning of wisdom'. 'Holy ones' (v. 3) is translated 'Holy One' in 9:10; we assume that in both verses the reference is to knowing God.

An object lesson from nature

In verse 4, there are five questions which any of us might ask when we look at the world and realize that we know very little of God's ways. In Job 38, similar questions are asked by God; here, God is the answer. To 'know someone's name and the name of their child' means to have an intimate acquaintance with them; Agur longs for a fuller revelation of God, a revelation that came fully only at the Incarnation.

The answer to the previous verse is that God has revealed himself, not only in nature but in his word, which is tried and tested ('proves true' is the term used for refining precious metals). This revelation brings more than knowledge; it encourages commitment—we can trust in God (v. 5). However, along with this reassurance comes a warning not to try to improve on what God has said (v. 6).

The Hebrew Bible is divided into three sections—the Law, the Prophets and the ' Writings', which in their completed form include Proverbs. By the time this chapter was written, the Law and most of the Prophets would be in place and so, probably, were the psalms.

Already the sin of trying to manipulate the scriptures is possible and must be avoided: 'You must neither add anything to what I command you nor take away anything from it, but keep the commandments of the Lord your God with which I am charging you' (Deuteronomy 4:2).

A twofold request

With the exception of verses 10, 17, 20 and 32–33, the rest of the chapter consists of 'numerical' Proverbs, where two, three or four things are mentioned—a way of expressing something indefinite, much as we say 'two or three' (see also 6:16–19 where 'six or seven' things which God hates are listed).

The first request (v. 8a) concerns character; it is a prayer for honesty and integrity. The second (vv. 8b–9) is rather more surprising. We might have expected either a prayer for prosperity as a sign of God's favour, which would be in line with the general thought of Proverbs, or at least for the ability to handle either wealth or poverty. But instead, what is asked is adequate but not lavish provision, for riches carry the danger of pride and self-sufficiency, while poverty can lead to theft, which would 'profane' or 'treat disrespectfully' God's name because it would mean breaking his commandment.

TO THINK ABOUT

As well as having an enquiring mind, Agur knows himself very well. He knows what he can and cannot handle, and prays accordingly. Self-knowledge can be painful, but it is also useful in helping us to avoid pitfalls and see the right way forward.

PRAYER

Lord, teach us how to pray aright,
With reverence and with fear;
Though dust and ashes in Thy sight,
We may, we must draw near.

James Montgomery (1771–1854)

MAKING TROUBLE

Slander (v. 10) is always a punishable offence, whether against a servant or anyone else. To 'wag the tongue' probably refers to unkind gossip to someone else about their staff—unwarranted meddling in other people's households. The servant's curse will be deserved and effective—it is only the undeserved curse that we need not fear (see 26:2). To 'be held guilty' or to 'incur guilt' is a technical term used of ritual offences (Leviticus 5:3; Numbers 5:6), and this is the only place where it is found in Proverbs. It is seriously wrong to make trouble for anybody, but particularly so when the target of our unkindness is in no position to retaliate, and does not even come under our authority.

Four faces of evil

'There are those' (v. 11) is actually 'there is a generation' or 'a circle' —people of a certain kind. It could be that one sin leads to another; first, there is disrespect of parents (v. 11), strongly condemned in Proverbs (see 20:20); then comes self-deception (v. 12), the self-right-eousness which boasts of ritual purity because certain ceremonies have been honoured, but which conceals rottenness at the core. 'Filthiness' is used here not in a physical but in a moral sense, as in Isaiah 4:4: '... once the Lord has washed away the filth of the daughters of Zion and cleansed the bloodstains of Jerusalem from its midst'.

Third, there is the sort of arrogance which is deaf to all correction (v. 13), and finally (v. 14) violent greed (the two words for 'teeth' are used in both a physical and a poetic sense), expressed in the unscrupulous use of power to gain one's own ends at the expense of the most unprotected members of society. The picture is of a danger-ous wild beast, hungry for prey and ready to snatch its victims whoever they are and wherever it finds them.

Never satisfied

The first part of verse 15 does not obviously relate to the second, unless it is to introduce the idea of permanent dissatisfaction, and to add 'two' to 'three and four'.

The leech is a bloodsucking creature; the picture is of two young leeches (either with identical names, or with identical cries) who like to cling to their chosen victims until they have had enough. Some people are like that, persistently demanding time and attention and requiring careful handling if they are not to wear out their chosen confidants.

The four things which are never satisfied (v. 16) are Sheol (see 27:20), which can never claim too many souls; the barren, or 'closed' womb (see Genesis 16:1), a reference to the desire of the childless for children—which remains strong, and leads to dilemmas about the advisability of fertility treatment and the ethics of surrogate motherhood; the ever-thirsty earth, which in Palestine is parched and dry except for the short rainy season; and the fire, which must constantly be fed if it is to keep alight. There is no moral to these verses; they state things as they are, and presumably are meant to broaden the readers' view of the world.

PRAYER

Lord, I know that none of the things about which I have just read are what you want. Make me clear-sighted when I am attracted by any of them, whether it is unkind gossip or greed and chronic discontentment, and help me to call on your Holy Spirit for help in those times of temptation.

HORROR in STORE

In verse 17, another of the 'odd' verses that are not connected with any of the numerical proverbs in the chapter, the theme of the disrespectful offspring which has recurred throughout the book (see 15:20; 20:20; 23:22) is summed up. Since contempt for parents is conveyed by a scornful look, the punishment is the loss of an eye in a horrible fashion. Vultures do not attack the living, so the picture here is of the undutiful child's dead body denied a burial (a disgrace in Israelite culture), thrown into a river bed, and consumed by birds of prey. Persistent sin eventually catches up with the sinner, even if it waits until the time of death.

Four wonderful things

Common to all four wonders (vv. 18–19) is the word 'way', but it is not easy to see any other connection. The first three all move without leaving a trace, and their means of propulsion are wonderful to see. They all master elements which are difficult—the air, the rock, the sea, and other people! But the likeliest interpretation is the simplest—'these are four marvels that are beyond me'. 'The way of a man with a girl' (v. 19) may refer to sexual intercourse, or to the miracle of birth which follows, or to the mysterious force which causes two people to fall in love. The word for 'girl' can mean either a virgin or simply a young woman.

A different way

Verse 20 is an isolated saying, probably placed here because it begins in the same way as verse 19. However, what it describes is anything but wonderful. The adulteress regards the act of adultery as no more significant than a meal, and sees no wrong in it. It is a shrewd comment on our capacity to deceive ourselves and to pass off our misdeeds as nothing to feel guilty about.

Four unbearable things

Verse 21 may be sarcastic—'the earth really totters under the burden of these characters'. They are all people of relatively humble position who come into power and influence and cannot handle them.

The slave can have no idea how to cope with the responsibilities of office, since he has only ever done as he is told. The fool (literally 'the scoffer', whose stupidity and obstinacy has an element of boorishness—see 9:7–8; 13:1; 15:12; 19:25; 21:11, 24; 22:10; 24:9) never knows when to stop. The 'unloved' or 'unsought' woman has to bear the stigma of being unmarried and then acquires a husband, and the maid 'succeeds' her mistress. A woman at that time would be unlikely to inherit property, but she might well supplant her mistress in the affections of the husband, and so virtually take her place in the household. All four situations have the potential for breeding arrogance, pretentiousness and conceited behaviour, and the examples are divided equally between the sexes.

TO THINK ABOUT

The world is full of marvels, and with these wonders comes the
possibility of spoiling it all. Have we always honoured our parents,
and never practised self-deceit when we have done wrong, or
behaved insufferably when we have had a piece of good fortune?
But while we pray to be kept from pride and self-deception, we can
still give thanks for the beauties of nature and the wonders of love.

PRAYER

Lord, help us to be both joyful and humble.

SMALL *but* WISE

Of the four small creatures mentioned here (vv. 24–28), the ant has already been commended for industry and foresight (6:6–8). The badger (a species of which lived in rock crevices) knows where to find safety. The locusts organize themselves with devastating effectiveness 'in rank' or 'detachments' without, apparently, even having a leader. The lizard is so small that one can pick it up, but its perseverance and capability are such that it can aspire to royal residences—a picture of audacity. The lesson is that it is not physical size and strength, but wisdom in the use of our abilities which counts in the search for success. Matthew Henry gives these verses a spiritual meaning when he comments, 'All that are wise to salvation are made wise by the grace of God.'

Stately in their stride

The first and the third of the 'stately' things are easy to understand— the 'king of beasts' (v. 30) and the nimble goat (v. 31). The other two are more difficult because the words are difficult to translate. The rooster (literally 'girt-about-the-loins', translated in various versions as greyhound, eagle, zebra and war-horse) is hardly an obvious example of dignity, though he has a distinctive gait. The king (v. 31) 'striding before his people' is in the nature of an educated guess, giving the picture of a king whose people are with him, and who can therefore lead them with confidence and without fear or anxiety. No moral is pointed here; this is simply an observation.

This is the last of the numerical proverbs; as well as being a literary device of the day, they may have something to say about the way in which God has ordered the world.

A call for humility and restraint

There has been a lot about pride and humility in this chapter; the final instruction (v. 32) to anyone guilty of arrogance or evil plans is to shut up!

Verse 33 illustrates what verse 32 urges, and is another plea for self-control and peaceable behaviour. Just as curd (v. 33) was produced by shaking milk in a bottle made of skin, and blood is drawn by pressing the nose, quarrelling and aggression come from encouraging (literally 'bringing forth') anger. There is a play on words here: the word for 'nose' is the same as that for 'anger', so 'the pressure on the nose brings blood; the pressure of anger brings bloodshed'.

Agur now disappears as suddenly as he arrived. What has he added to the teaching of Proverbs?

He is a keen observer of the natural world, and is acutely aware of its wonders and of the lessons which we can draw from it. He is a humble man, whose request to God is both modest and moderate (vv. 7–8). Like the other writers, he hates gossip (v. 10), greed (vv. 15–16) and above all pride and self-deception (vv. 11, 14, 17, 21–22, 32). These and other sins, if they are indulged rather than checked (v. 33), lead to bitterness and strife.

TO THINK ABOUT

It may be that Agur, who has no great opinion of himself (vv. 2–3), has learnt these lessons the hard way. We would be well advised to profit from his experience, and at the same time remember that his diffidence does not diminish the authority of his words, for
'all scripture is inspired by God and is useful for teaching, for reproof, for correction, and for training in righteousness'
(2 Timothy 3:16).

PRAYER

Lord, show me how I can learn from the experience of others which I read in your word.

KING LEMUEL & HIS MOTHER

Verse 1 is the only piece of advice in Proverbs which is addressed specifically to a king, and attributed to his mother. Lemuel was not a king of Israel, although his name is Hebrew for 'belonging to God'. If we read 'King Lemuel. An oracle' as 'Lemuel, king of Massa' (see 30:1), this would place him in north-west Arabia.

The queen mother had some considerable say at court in the Bible, as in the rest of the ancient Near East. There is the sad comment on King Azariah of Judah whose mother Athaliah 'was his counsellor in doing wickedly' (2 Chronicles 22:3)—a reasonable judgment when we read her story in 2 Kings 11.

Lemuel's mother advises her son on what is expected of him, and the advice, though limited, is sensible.

A strong plea

'No!' (v. 2) is translated in some other versions as 'What?' in the sense of 'What shall I say to you?' (so REB, RSV and KJV). Clearly the mother is concerned for her son: he is 'the son of her vows'—a term used for a child given because vows are made, as in the story of Hannah and Samuel (1 Samuel 1)—and therefore specially precious, and she is vehement in her desire that he shall avoid what is wrong.

What to avoid

First, destructive relationships with undesirable and untrustworthy women (v. 3)—a theme which is dealt with in chapters 2, 5—7 and 9. Second, there is the danger of drunkenness (v. 4). It is unlikely that total abstinence would be a rule at the royal Courts of the time, but the Wisdom writers are aware of the dangers of excess (see 23:29–30). The reason for this advice is that loose living affects the wits and damages the powers of judgment (v. 5), so that the king will ignore or even pervert the law, particularly when dealing with the 'afflicted' (literally 'bowed down' with poverty and oppression). This is not what is expected of him.

A case for getting drunk?

It is difficult to know whether verses 6 and 7 are serious or cynical. If they are serious, they are saying that strong drink has its uses, however temporarily, in dulling the misery of the wretched. If they are cynical, they are a reminder to the ruler that he has better things to do than drown his sorrows.

What to do

The first thing to do is to 'speak out' (v. 8). Those who, because of poverty or fear, are unable to speak for themselves, and the 'destitute' (literally 'those who are passing away' or 'those who are left behind'—probably orphans and others who have no protection), need a bold and powerful advocate. The second thing is not only to speak, but to act (v. 9): the poor and needy are entitled to justice, and it is the king who administers it. These verses apply to us today. We have a duty to speak for those whose voice is never heard, and, like the Old Testament king, to work on their behalf for justice.

The psalmist says to the king:

In your majesty ride on victoriously
  for the cause of truth and to defend the right (Psalm 45:4).

TO THINK ABOUT

Proverbs has a lot of time for the wisdom of the older generation, and this last piece of advice, so loving and so down to earth, has something to say about what their experience can contribute to our lives, if we will hear them.

PRAYER

Lord, give me the patience and humility to listen to those who are older than me, and to think seriously about what they have to say.

108 PROVERBS 31:10–31

An A *to* Z *of* EXCELLENCE (1)

These twenty-two verses are an acrostic—each begins with a letter of the Hebrew alphabet, a device found elsewhere in the Old Testament (see Psalm 119), perhaps making the passage easy to learn, perhaps expressing the wholeness both of the description and of the subject itself. However, this way of writing makes it difficult, if not impossible, for thoughts to be expressed in a logical sequence, so one way of making sense of the passage is to look for any themes which are scattered throughout it.

The setting is a comfortable, middle-class home, not royal or aristocratic, but prosperous and secure—the kind of establishment which we would expect to be the reward of the hard work and integrity described throughout Proverbs (see, for example, 28:19–20).

The central figure is not, as elsewhere, the farmer or the shepherd or the king or even the master of the house, but the wife and mother. She is capable—literally 'a woman of strength' (v. 10; see 12:4 and Ruth 3:11) and she is able to manage not only her family and her household, but also business interests of her own.

Family life

This woman is more precious than jewels, because she is irreplaceable (v. 10). She has her husband's trust and confidence (v. 11), and their partnership and the commitment which go with it are lifelong (v. 12). Himself a prominent and respected citizen (v. 23), he speaks of her with unqualified praise and admiration (v. 29); these words must be his, since they alone in the chapter are addressed directly to her.

Husband and children 'rise up' (an expression used of someone about to make a considered statement) and call her 'happy', or 'blessed' (vv. 27–28)—the happiness which elsewhere is associated with a right relationship with God and others:

> *Happy are those*
> *who do not follow the advice of the wicked...*
> *but their delight is in the law of the Lord* (Psalm 1:1–2).

Domestic life

She has a considerable household to manage—meals have to be organized and 'tasks' given to the servant girls (v. 15), and she is able and conscientious (v. 27). She is not afraid of hard work: 'girding herself' (v. 17) probably refers to the custom of tucking the skirts of a long robe into a belt to allow free movement when there is a heavy task to be faced. She gets up early (v. 15) and goes to bed late (v. 18b)—keeping a lamp burning all night may mean that this is a prosperous set-up, but may also be the equivalent of 'burning the midnight oil'. Perhaps because of the family's prosperity, but more likely because of her own foresight, she is well prepared for life's ups and downs, and she and her household are warmly clad (vv. 21–22). 'Crimson' (v. 21) can indicate luxury, but the word is in a form which means 'double', so in the context of cold weather it may be referring to the double-thickness of the clothing she supplies.

Business life

This woman is not only in charge of her own establishment, she has a successful career (v. 18a). As well as making clothes (v. 19), she sells them, and apparently takes orders for 'sashes' or girdles for the merchants with whom she deals (v. 24)—perhaps those from whom she buys imported goods (v. 14). She is also active in buying and selling land—an enterprise usually reserved for men—and is involved in the negotiations which lead to a satisfactory purchase (v. 16). Her abilities are recognized; the opinion is that she should be allowed to profit from her enterprises, and—perhaps the ultimate tribute—she is spoken well of in the 'city gates', the meeting place of the men who are the local leaders (v. 31).

TO THINK ABOUT

Is this the first example of 'having it all'? It certainly counter-balances the early descriptions of the adulteress in Proverbs, to some extent correcting its ambivalent attitude towards women, and opens up the traditional role of the wife and mother to areas well outside the home. But the success, as we shall see, is built not on measurable achievement but on a secure personality and loving relationships.

An A to Z of Excellence (11)

The picture so far has been of almost frightening efficiency, tempered by the love and affection which go with a successful marriage and a happy family life.

What is she like as a person?

She has an inner security which is seen in the poise and dignity which she wears like a garment. From the same source comes serenity in contemplating the future—she is not a worrier (v. 25). When she speaks, it is with both wisdom and kindness (the word sometimes translated 'faithfulness' or 'steadfast love') (v. 26).

Verse 30 indicates that her inner strength is not dependent on beauty and charm, for the one can be misleading and the other fades quite soon. The key to excellence is in the 'fear of the Lord'—a life lived in the loving and reverent obedience to him which is 'the beginning of wisdom' (1:7).

Is this all too good to be true? If, as has been suggested, this is a handbook for prospective brides or bridegrooms, it is somewhat intimidating. Who can achieve half that this paragon of virtue, industry and creativity manages? Who can fail to be disappointed in a partner if this is the standard that is expected?

One answer is that this is an ideal to admire and strive for, rather than an enquiry into our own capabilities. The best is set before us, and we should not, women or men, aspire to anything less, even though we achieve only a lesser standard.

Wisdom incarnate?

Another possibility is that this description of the capable wife can also be interpreted in a spiritual sense. In Proverbs 8:22 we have a picture of Wisdom present with God before the world began, and working with him at the creation. Is it possible that here we have the corresponding picture of Wisdom incarnate, the loving, generous, creative force which is the evidence of God's presence in the world? And if so, is this gift available to us? The New Testament has no doubt about the answer: 'If any of you is lacking in wisdom, ask God... But ask in faith, never doubting' (James 1:5–6).

Wisdom is the theme of Proverbs, connecting life in the family, at Court, in business and agriculture. Wisdom must be our guiding principle if we are to live upright, just, merciful and honest lives. No matter is too small for Wisdom to be involved, from the disciplining of children to the avoidance of excess. Nothing is too great, for she is inseparable from God and from his work. But we cannot learn her secrets by our own unaided efforts; if we try, we shall become demoralized and discouraged by failure. Only our relationship with God himself can ensure that we share in this aspect of his nature. So Proverbs ends as it began, with 'the fear of the Lord' which is 'the beginning of wisdom' (v. 30; 1:7).

TO THINK ABOUT

The standards set by these verses, like those set by the whole book, are very high. Yet they apply throughout to ordinary people like us, and there is nothing here that we cannot achieve if we live a life of obedience to God.

PRAYER

We ask of thee the wisdom that cometh from above, which is pure and peaceable, without partiality and without hypocrisy. Teach us to think soberly of ourselves, as we ought to think, and to bear each other's burdens always. Make us fruitful in every good work, to do thy will; through Jesus Christ our Lord.
(James 3:17; Titus 2:12; Colossians 1:10, adapted)

NOTES

NOTES

NOTES

NOTES

NOTES

NOTES

NOTES

NOTES

NOTES

NOTES

NOTES

NOTES

NOTES

NOTES

NOTES

NOTES

NOTES

NOTES

NOTES

NOTES

NOTES